Life in the UK Test
Practice Questions

Questions and answers for the British citizenship test

Published by Red Squirrel Publishing

Red Squirrel Publishing
Suite 235, 77 Beak Street,
London W1F 9DB, United Kingdom

www.redsquirrelbooks.com

First edition published in 2006
Fifth edition – Second impression

A list of known errors or corrections is published at
www.redsquirrelbooks.com/errata

ISBN: 978-1-907389-28-3

Edited by Henry Dillon and George Sandison
Assisted by Suzanne Connelly

Proofreading by Robert Clarke

Designed and artworked by Cox Design Limited, Witney, Oxon

Printed and bound in Aberwystwyth by Cambrian

CONTENTS

Introduction 5

Questions to Expect 9

Practice Test 1 13

Practice Test 2 19

Practice Test 3 25

Practice Test 4 31

Practice Test 5 37

Practice Test 6 43

Practice Test 7 49

Practice Test 8 55

Practice Test 9 61

Practice Test 10 67

Practice Test 11 73

Practice Test 12 79

Practice Test 13 85

Practice Test 14 91

Practice Test 15 97

Practice Test 16 103

Practice Test 17 109

Practice Test 18 115

Practice Test 19 121

Practice Test 20 127

INTRODUCTION

The Life in the UK Test is an essential part of the process for anyone planning on becoming a British citizen or applying for Indefinite Leave to Remain. Passing the test is compulsory under the 'Knowledge of life and language in the UK' requirement of your application.

You must do two things to meet this requirement:

- pass the Life in the UK test, AND
- have a speaking and listening qualification in English at B1 CEFR or higher, or its equivalent

Some exemptions to these requirements apply. For instance, if you have a degree-level qualification, or higher, taught in English you do not have to pass an English language test. You are also exempt if you are from a majority English speaking country.

Over 150,000 people take the Life in the UK Test every year, but not all of them pass. With each attempt costing £50, this can be an expensive mistake. However, with the right preparation, you can be one of those who passes first time.

About this book

This book is designed to test your knowledge and understanding of the official study materials. This introduction offers advice on how to prepare for the test and guidance on the kinds of question you will face in your test.

There are 20 complete practice tests, each containing 24 questions in the same format as the actual test. The questions are all based on the testable sections of the official study materials, and these are the following chapters:

- The values and principles of the UK
- What is the UK?
- A long and illustrious history
- A modern, thriving society
- The UK government, the law and your role.

Take some time to read through the following sections carefully. They tell you about all the features of this book and will enable you to get as much out of it as possible.

Page references

The answer tables for each practice test include a page reference to the 2015 study materials. They refer to our books, *Life in the UK Test: Handbook 2015* (ISBN: 978-1-907389-29-0), *Life in the UK Test: Study Guide 2015* (ISBN: 978-1-907389-26-9) and *Life in the UK Test: Study Guide & CD ROM 2015* (ISBN: 978-1-907389-27-6).

These page references tell you exactly which bit of the official study materials each question is based on. You can use these to revise difficult topics and target your study.

How to prepare for the test

1. Study the materials

The first and most important step of your preparations is to study the complete official study materials. These are found in the Home Office handbook, *Life in the United Kingdom: A guide for new residents* and are reproduced in our titles, *Life in the UK Test: Study Guide* and *Handbook*. You can find more information about these books at **www.lifeintheuk.net/studyguide**

It is essential that you read and understand the testable chapters before taking your test. Taking practice tests alone will not prepare you for the real test.

2. Take practice tests

Once you've finished thoroughly reviewing the study materials, you should check if you are ready to take the test by completing the practice tests from this book.

When you sit your official test, you will be given 45 minutes to complete the test. So when you take a practice test, you should allow yourself the same time. The pass mark in the official test is at least 75% – or only six incorrect answers. Again, this is what you should aim to score when you take a practice test.

If you can consistently score at least 75% and finish a test within 45 minutes, then you are ready to take your official test.

If you do not pass the practice tests satisfactorily and do not feel confident enough to sit your official test you should continue your study of the testable materials. If you do not have sufficient time left before your official test to do more study, then you may be able to reschedule your test appointment. You can reschedule your test without charge up to seven days before the date. If you cancel your booking with less than seven days' notice, your booking fee will not be refunded.

3. Online tests

Once you've finished testing yourself using the questions in this book, you can go online and access further tests with our free subscription offer.

Visit **www.lifeintheuk.net/test** and register an account to redeem this offer.

WARNING: DO NOT MEMORISE QUESTIONS

The practice questions contained in this book are intended to help you assess your understanding of the study materials and check if you are ready to take the official test.

Do not prepare for the test by memorising the questions in this book.

All the questions are in the same format as the official test questions. But they are not identical to the questions in the official test. The Home Office regularly revises the wording of questions used in the Life in the UK Test.

It is very important that you fully read and understand the study materials before taking your test.

SEND US YOUR FEEDBACK

Our books have helped thousands of people pass the Life in the UK Test. So we're always delighted when we hear from our readers. You can send us your comments by visiting **www.lifeintheuk.net/feedback**

CHECKLIST

There are a lot of things that you need to remember to do for the Life in the UK Test. Avoid problems and get organised by completing this checklist.

☐ Test appointment booked

Book your test through the Life in the UK Test booking website **www.lituktestbooking.co.uk** or by calling the Life in the UK Test Helpline on **0800 015 4245**

Test Date .... Time ....

Test Centre Address ....

....

....

Phone ....

☐ Finished reading study materials

☐ Completed all practice tests in this book

☐ Completed free online practice tests at **www.lifeintheuk.net**

☐ Checked latest tips and advice at **www.lifeintheuk.net**

☐ Checked your registered details exactly match your photo ID

☐ Checked your proof of address is valid

☐ Confirmed test centre location and travel route

QUESTIONS TO EXPECT

All questions in the Life in the UK Test are multiple-choice. There are four different formats in which a question may be asked:

1. One correct answer – Choose the correct answer to the question from four options

EXAMPLE

What important event in the development of women's rights happened in 1928?

- **A** Women were first given the right to vote
- **B** Women were given the right to vote at the same age as men
- **C** The first divorce laws were introduced
- **D** Women were allowed to keep their own earnings and property

2. Two correct answers – Choose two correct answers to the question from four options

EXAMPLE

Which TWO of the following are famous Paralympians?

- **A** Baroness Tanni Grey-Thompson
- **B** Dame Kelly Holmes
- **C** Jayne Torvill
- **D** Ellie Simmonds

3. True or false – Decide whether a statement is true or false

EXAMPLE

Is the statement below TRUE or FALSE?
A newspaper's owner may try to influence government policy by running a campaign.

- **A** True
- **B** False

4. Select correct statement – Choose the correct statement from two options

EXAMPLE

Which of these statements is correct?

A Florence Nightingale is often regarded as the founder of modern nursing.

B Florence Nightingale pioneered the use of syringes in hospitals.

Working through the answers

When you start your test, make sure you read each question carefully. Make sure you understand it.

If you are confident that you know the correct answer, make your selection and move on to the next question.

It is vital that you select an answer for every question even if you are not confident that it is correct. There is a chance that even a guess will be correct! If you do this, make sure that you note the question number on your blank paper. It is possible that a question later in the test will help you to answer a question that you have found difficult.

Traps to watch out for

Some questions may be worded so that an option may be a TRUE statement but not the CORRECT answer to the question being asked.

Be careful if questions and answers use words that are absolute. These words mean that the question or answer applies in all cases (e.g. *always*, *every*) or not at all (e.g. *never*).

EXAMPLE

Which of the following statements is correct?

A There are a few members of Parliament who do not represent any of the main political parties.

B All members of Parliament have to belong to a political party.

The second statement is absolute. There are no exceptions. This means the correct answer is A because, whether or not there are currently independent members of Parliament (MPs) in Parliament, there *can* be independent MPs in Parliament.

You also need to be careful of words that *moderate* a question or answer. When words such as *often, rarely, sometimes* and *usually* are used, this means that the question or answer is referring to something that is not true in all cases.

EXAMPLE

Who usually chooses who will be the Archbishop of Canterbury?

- **A** The monarch
- **B** The Prime Minister and a committee appointed by the Church
- **C** A committee appointed by the Church
- **D** The Prime Minister

In the above example, all of the options could be correct. The monarch has the right to choose, but does not in practice. A committee appointed by the Church and the Prime Minister are both usually involved in the decision. This means that C and D are accurate, but not correct because they don't provide a full answer. B is the only answer that fully answers the question.

Also watch for negative words in questions or answers – such as *not, never* and *neither.* These words can be easily overlooked and completely change the meaning of the question being asked.

EXAMPLE

Which of these socially progressive measures was NOT introduced during the early years of the 20th century?

- **A** Free school meals
- **B** Old-age pensions
- **C** Financial help for the unemployed
- **D** Equal pay for women

In the example above, notice that the question is asking for the statement that is not correct. Free school meals, old-age pensions and financial help for the unemployed were all introduced at the start of the 20th century. There are no laws enforcing equal pay conditions for women in the UK, however. Therefore, although option D is a false statement, it is the correct answer for this question.

For some questions, one of the answers may read: 'All of the above'. In these cases, read the other answers carefully to see if it is possible that they are all correct. Even if two of the three answers seem correct, all three alternative answers must be correct for you to choose the 'all of the above' option.

For some questions, one of the answers may read: 'None of the above'. In these cases, read the other answers carefully to see if it is possible that they are all incorrect. Even if two of the three answers seem incorrect, all three alternative answers must be wrong for you to choose the 'none of the above' option.

Dates

The study materials say that, 'Questions are based on ALL parts of the handbook, but you will not need to remember dates of birth or death' (see *The values and principles of the UK*). This means that whilst you won't have to quote specific dates, you must understand when key events happened, or when certain individuals lived. For example, you will not be asked a question such as 'What year was Isaac Newton born in?', though you could be asked 'Which scientist, born in 1643, discovered that white light is made up of the colours of the rainbow?'

PRACTICE TEST 1

1 Which of the following statements is correct?

- **A** Many civilian volunteers in small boats from Britain helped the British Navy to rescue more than 300,000 men from the beaches around Dunkirk.
- **B** 300,000 men were rescued from the beaches around Dunkirk solely by British Navy ships.

2 How old was Edward VI when he died?

- **A** 15
- **B** 18
- **C** 56
- **D** 35

3 Scotland changed in which TWO ways after the Battle of Culloden?

- **A** Chieftains became landlords if they had the favour of the English king
- **B** Chieftains took control of the land away from the English king
- **C** Clansmen became tenants who had to pay for the land they used
- **D** The clans were entirely destroyed

4 Which of the following statements is correct?

- **A** A bank holiday in the UK refers to all the banks being closed on that day.
- **B** A bank holiday in the UK happens each calendar month.

5 Which TWO of the following are famous British landmarks?

- **A** The London Eye
- **B** Albert Square
- **C** The Eden Project
- **D** The Smithsonian

6 Which country of the UK is NOT represented on the Union Flag?

- **A** Scotland
- **B** Wales
- **C** Northern Ireland
- **D** England

7 Which of these people was a great British playwright?

- **A** Sir Francis Drake
- **B** Geoffrey Chaucer
- **C** William Caxton
- **D** William Shakespeare

8 Which of these statements is correct?

- **A** Refuges and shelters offer a safe place to stay for victims of domestic violence.
- **B** The Citizens Advice Bureau offers a safe place to stay for victims of domestic violence.

9 When were the first professional football clubs formed?

- **A** The Middle Ages
- **B** 17th Century
- **C** 19th Century
- **D** 20th Century

10 Which work of music did Benjamin Britten NOT write?

- **A** *Peter Grimes*
- **B** *The Planets*
- **C** *Billy Budd*
- **D** *A Young Person's Guide to the Orchestra*

11 Which of the following countries did NOT help to set up the EEC?

- **A** Ireland
- **B** Luxemburg
- **C** Belgium
- **D** Germany

12 Which of the following is a good way of helping your community?

- **A** Travelling
- **B** Complaining
- **C** Volunteering
- **D** Spending lots of time online

13 How are local authorities funded?

- **A** By funding from central government only
- **B** By taxation only
- **C** By central government funding and by taxation
- **D** Local authorities are unfunded

14 Is the statement below TRUE or FALSE?
Discrimination in the workplace is an example of criminal law.

- **A** True
- **B** False

15 Which of these statements is correct?

- **A** Everyone pays National Insurance Contributions.
- **B** Most working people pay National Insurance Contributions.

16 Whom did William the Conqueror defeat at the Battle of Hastings in 1066?

- **A** King Cnut
- **B** Boudicca
- **C** Kenneth MacAlpin
- **D** King Harold

17 Which British novelist created the fictional detective, Sherlock Holmes?

- **A** Sir Arthur Conan Doyle
- **B** Evelyn Waugh
- **C** Robert Louis Stevenson
- **D** Graham Greene

18 The judiciary is responsible for which TWO of the following?

- **A** Interpreting the law
- **B** Making the law
- **C** Arresting people
- **D** Making sure that trials are fair

19 Who chairs debates in the House of Commons?

- **A** The leader of the opposition
- **B** The Prime Minister
- **C** The Speaker
- **D** The Foreign Secretary

20 Which of these is an accurate estimate of the number of casualties suffered by Britain in the First World War?

- **A** 2 million
- **B** 10 million
- **C** 8 million
- **D** 500,000

21 William Shakespeare wrote a number of sonnets. What are sonnets?

- **A** Poems of 14 lines
- **B** Mystery plays
- **C** Rhyming poems
- **D** Stories for children

22 Is the statement below TRUE or FALSE?
Population growth in the UK has been faster in recent years, thanks in part to migration and longer life expectancy.

- **A** True
- **B** False

23 How old do you have to be to buy alcohol in the UK?

- **A** 16
- **B** 18
- **C** 20
- **D** 21

24 Who is the patron saint of Scotland?

- **A** St David
- **B** St George
- **C** St Patrick
- **D** St Andrew

ANSWERS: PRACTICE TEST 1

			Study material reference
1	A	Many civilian volunteers in small boats from Britain helped the British Navy to rescue more than 300,000 men from the beaches around Dunkirk.	p48–51
2	A	15	p22–4
3	A	Chieftains became landlords if they had the favour of the English king	p34–5
	C	Clansmen became tenants who had to pay for the land they used	
4	A	A bank holiday in the UK refers to all the banks being closed on that day.	p73
5	A	The London Eye	p95–103
	C	The Eden Project	
6	B	Wales	p40
7	D	William Shakespeare	p26
8	A	Refuges and shelters offer a safe place to stay for victims of domestic violence.	p136
9	C	19th Century	p76–7
10	B	*The Planets*	p79–81
11	A	Ireland	p124–5
12	C	Volunteering	p141
13	C	By central government funding and by taxation	p115
14	B	False	p126–7
15	B	Most working people pay National Insurance Contributions.	p138–9
16	D	King Harold	p15–6
17	A	Sir Arthur Conan Doyle	p86
18	A	Interpreting the law	p129–30
	D	Making sure that trials are fair	
19	C	The Speaker	p111–2
20	A	2 million	p46–7
21	A	Poems of 14 lines	p86–8
22	A	True	p64–5
23	B	18	p126–7
24	D	St Andrew	p67–8

PRACTICE TEST 2

1 Which TWO of the following are British values based on?

- **A** Traditions
- **B** EU law
- **C** Party politics
- **D** History

2 MPs have a duty to serve and represent which of the following groups?

- **A** Their fellow MPs
- **B** Everyone in their constituency
- **C** Everyone in their constituency who voted for them
- **D** The House of Lords

3 Which of the following statements is correct?

- **A** During the Industrial Revolution canals were built to link the mines in the mountains with factories in the cities.
- **B** During the Industrial Revolution canals were built to link the factories to cities and ports.

4 An attempt by which group to put James II's son on the throne instead of George I was quickly defeated?

- **A** French Huguenots
- **B** Scottish Jacobites
- **C** Irish Catholics
- **D** English Puritans

5 Is the statement below TRUE or FALSE?
The Bill of Rights confirmed the rights of Parliament and the limits of the king's power.

A True

B False

6 Charles I was unwilling to reach an agreement with Parliament. Following his defeat in the Civil war, what happened to him?

A He was exiled

B He was executed

C He was exonerated

D He was excommunicated

7 Is the statement below TRUE or FALSE?
Following the Emancipation Act of 1833, the Royal Navy stopped slave ships from other countries and freed the slaves.

A True

B False

8 Is the statement below TRUE or FALSE?
Lands taken from Catholics in 17th century Ireland and given to Protestant settlers were known as 'plantations'.

A True

B False

9 Which of the following provide legal advice, normally for a fee?

A Judges

B Magistrates

C Solicitors

D The police

10 Is the statement below TRUE or FALSE?
Some people rent land away from home called an allotment, where they can grow fruit and vegetables.

A True

B False

11 Which of these statements is true?

A Most people live in towns and cities but much of Britain is still countryside.

B Most people live in the countryside but much of Britain is covered by towns and cities.

12 During the reign of Henry VIII, which country of the union became formally united with England?

A Ireland

B Wales

C Scotland

D Northern Ireland

13 What sport is played in the UEFA Champions League?

A Tennis

B Rugby

C Football

D Cricket

14 Is the statement below TRUE or FALSE?
Norman French influenced the development of the English language as we know it today.

A True

B False

15 Which of the following statements is correct?

- **A** The attack on Normandy by Allied forces is often called D-Day.
- **B** D-Day was an Allied operation that attacked German forces in France by advancing through Spain.

16 Which annual flower show in London exhibits garden designs from around the world?

- **A** South Bank
- **B** Covent Garden
- **C** Chelsea
- **D** Kensington

17 Where did the people of the Bronze Age bury their dead?

- **A** Wheelbarrows
- **B** Round barrows
- **C** Burial mounds
- **D** Hill forts

18 The right for every adult male and female to vote is usually known as what?

- **A** Universal balloting
- **B** Universal democracy
- **C** Universal voting rights
- **D** Universal suffrage

19 What event in 1851 took place at the Crystal Palace in Hyde Park and showed goods and exhibits from Britain and across the world?

- **A** The Great Exhibition
- **B** The Great Show
- **C** The Great Event
- **D** The Great Occasion

20 Sake Dean Mahomet opened which establishment in George Street, London in 1810?

- **A** Hindoostane Coffee House
- **B** Pakistan Curry House
- **C** Mahomet Coffee House
- **D** Mahomet Shampoo Parlour

21 Which of these is NOT a Christmas tradition in the UK?

- **A** Giving gifts
- **B** Having a barbecue
- **C** Sending cards
- **D** Decorating houses and trees

22 Catherine Parr married Henry VIII late in his life. Who died first?

- **A** She died first and he never remarried
- **B** He died first and she was a widow for the rest of her life
- **C** She died in childbirth and Henry remarried
- **D** He died first and she went on to remarry

23 Which of the following statements is correct?

- **A** Elizabeth I came to the throne when, following a short reign, her half-sister Mary died.
- **B** Elizabeth I came to the throne when, following a long reign, her cousin Mary died.

24 Who wrote musicals such as *Cats, The Phantom of the Opera* and *Evita*?

- **A** Sir Edward Elgar
- **B** Gilbert and Sullivan
- **C** Andrew Lloyd Webber
- **D** Julian Lloyd Webber

ANSWERS: PRACTICE TEST 2

			Study material reference
1	A	Traditions	p2–3
	D	History	
2	B	Everyone in their constituency	p112
3	B	During the Industrial Revolution canals were built to link the factories to cities and ports.	p35–7
4	B	Scottish Jacobites	p34
5	A	True	p33
6	B	He was executed	p28–30
7	A	True	p37–8
8	A	True	p27
9	C	Solicitors	p134–5
10	A	True	p88–9
11	A	Most people live in towns and cities but much of Britain is still countryside.	p62
12	B	Wales	p22–4
13	C	Football	p76–7
14	A	True	p15–6
15	A	The attack on Normandy by Allied forces is often called D-Day.	p48–51
16	C	Chelsea	p84–5
17	B	Round barrows	p12–3
18	D	Universal suffrage	p43–4
19	A	The Great Exhibition	p41–2
20	A	Hindoostane Coffee House	p37
21	B	Having a barbecue	p69–71
22	D	He died first and she went on to remarry	p23
23	A	Elizabeth I came to the throne when, following a short reign, her half-sister Mary died.	p22–4
24	C	Andrew Lloyd Webber	p81–2

PRACTICE TEST 3

1 **Which of the following statements is correct?**

- **A** The Wimbledon Championships are associated with athletics.
- **B** The Wimbledon Championships are associated with tennis.

2 **The last successful foreign invasion of England was by which of the following?**

- **A** The Romans led by Julius Caeser
- **B** The Romans led by Emperor Claudius
- **C** The Vikings
- **D** The Normans led by William

3 **Is the statement below TRUE or FALSE?**
Mary Peters was an author who was later made a Dame in recognition of her work promoting literacy.

- **A** True
- **B** False

4 **Where does the UK Parliament sit?**

- **A** Westminster
- **B** Downing Street
- **C** Stormont
- **D** The House of Lords

5 **Which of the following statements is correct?**

- **A** The 'Divine Right of Kings' was the view held by many English monarchs that they could seize lands belonging to the nobility as they wished.
- **B** The 'Divine Right of Kings' was the view held by many English monarchs that they were directly appointed by God to rule.

6 The repeal of the Corn Laws in 1846 was designed to do what?

- **A** Allow the import of cheap grain
- **B** Encourage British farmers to grow more grain
- **C** Increase the quality of bread
- **D** Introduce more efficient working practices on British farms

7 The Wars of the Roses was fought by the supporters of which TWO families in order to decide who should be King of England?

- **A** The House of Lancaster
- **B** The House of Windsor
- **C** The House of York
- **D** The House of Tudor

8 Which famous leader said the following:
'We shall fight on the beaches, we shall fight on the landing grounds, we shall fight in the fields and in the streets, we shall fight in the hills; we shall never surrender.'

- **A** Admiral Nelson
- **B** Winston Churchill
- **C** Clement Attlee
- **D** Oliver Cromwell

9 Which of the following statements is correct?

- **A** The police must always obey the law, except when investigating a difficult case.
- **B** The police must always obey the law.

10 Which of the following is NOT an aim of the United Nations?

- **A** To promote peace
- **B** To promote international security
- **C** To prevent war
- **D** To promote free trade

11 How often is a General Election held?

- **A** Every year
- **B** At least every two years
- **C** At least every four years
- **D** At least every five years

12 After his campaign in Ireland and his defeat of Charles II, Oliver Cromwell was given what title?

- **A** King
- **B** Lord Lieutenant
- **C** Lord Protector
- **D** Chieftain

13 Which of the following statements is correct?

- **A** The Black Death destroyed cereal crops, leading to a famine which killed many peasants.
- **B** After the Black Death there were labour shortages and peasants began to demand higher wages.

14 What is the capital city of Northern Ireland?

- **A** Belfast
- **B** Dublin
- **C** The Pale
- **D** Edinburgh

15 What is New Year's Eve called in Scotland?

- **A** Boxing Day
- **B** Hogmanay
- **C** Auld Lang Syne
- **D** St Andrew's Day

16 Who or what were the 'clans'?

- **A** English lords
- **B** Welsh landowners
- **C** Prominent families in Scotland and Ireland
- **D** Prominent families in England and Wales

17 Who was James II's eldest daughter, Mary, married to?

- **A** William of Orange
- **B** The Duke of York
- **C** The French Dauphin
- **D** She never married

18 Britain was brought into conflict with which country during the 19th century, because they were expanding and trading in similar areas?

- **A** Germany
- **B** The Netherlands
- **C** Spain
- **D** France

19 Which 1935 film was directed by Alfred Hitchcock?

- **A** *The 21 Steps*
- **B** *The 39 Steps*
- **C** *The 100 Steps*
- **D** *The 1,001 Steps*

20 Is the statement below TRUE or FALSE?
Members of the House of Lords are elected by a constituency.

- **A** True
- **B** False

21 Who wrote the novel *Lucky Jim*?

- **A** James Joyce
- **B** Sir Kingsley Amis
- **C** James Callaghan
- **D** Jimmy Tarbuck

22 Which of these statements is correct?

- **A** The United Kingdom consists of England, Ireland, Scotland and Wales.
- **B** The United Kingdom consists of England, Scotland, Wales and Northern Ireland.

23 Which TWO of the following are amongst the shared goals of the Commonwealth?

- **A** Development
- **B** Dependency
- **C** Democracy
- **D** Discrimination

24 Which of the following is one of the Queen's important ceremonial roles?

- **A** To chair debates in Parliament
- **B** To write laws
- **C** To receive foreign ambassadors and high commissioners
- **D** To negotiate trade agreements with other countries

ANSWERS: PRACTICE TEST 3

			Study material reference
1	B	The Wimbledon Championships are associated with tennis.	p78
2	D	The Normans led by William	p15–6
3	B	False	p57
4	A	Westminster	p8
5	B	The 'Divine Right of Kings' was the view held by many English monarchs that they were directly appointed by God to rule.	p27–8
6	A	Allow the import of cheap grain	p41–2
7	A	The House of Lancaster	p21
	C	The House of York	
8	B	Winston Churchill	p50
9	B	The police must always obey the law.	p127–8
10	D	To promote free trade	p125
11	D	At least every five years	p112
12	C	Lord Protector	p28–30
13	B	After the Black Death there were labour shortages and peasants began to demand higher wages.	p17–8
14	A	Belfast	p63
15	B	Hogmanay	p35
16	C	Prominent families in Scotland and Ireland	p17–8
17	A	William of Orange	p31–2
18	D	France	p35–7
19	B	*The 39 Steps*	p91
20	B	False	p111
21	B	Sir Kingsley Amis	p86
22	B	The United Kingdom consists of England, Scotland, Wales and Northern Ireland.	p8
23	A	Development	p123
	C	Democracy	
24	C	To receive foreign ambassadors and high commissioners	p107–9

PRACTICE TEST 4

1 Is the statement below TRUE or FALSE?
Under the system of feudalism, the kings gave land to lords, and the landowners had to send men to serve in the army in return.

A True

B False

2 Is a verdict of 'not proven' possible?

A Yes, but only in a Magistrates' Court

B Yes, but only in Scotland

3 Is the statement below TRUE or FALSE?
Jane Austen and Charles Dickens were both famous sculptors.

A True

B False

4 Which of the following is NOT a name for an EU law?

A Directive

B Diktat

C Framework decision

D Regulation

5 Is the statement below TRUE or FALSE?
Adult citizens of other EU states may vote in General Elections.

A True

B False

6 After the Act of Union, Scotland was no longer an independent country. In what ways was it still separate from the rest of Great Britain?

- **A** Hadrian's Wall stopped people travelling freely
- **B** It kept its own educational system
- **C** No one spoke English
- **D** It had its own monarch

7 Which of the following statements is correct?

- **A** A dog's owner is responsible for keeping the animal under control and cleaning up after it in public places.
- **B** A dog's owner is responsible for keeping it under control, but doesn't have to clean up after it in public places.

8 Is the statement below TRUE or FALSE?
Richard Arkwright developed horse-driven spinning mills that used only one machine, increasing efficiency and production.

- **A** True
- **B** False

9 Which of these books did Graham Greene NOT write?

- **A** *The Honorary Consul*
- **B** *Brighton Rock*
- **C** *Moby Dick*
- **D** *The Heart of the Matter*

10 Who were Elizabeth I's parents?

- **A** Henry VII and Elizabeth of York
- **B** Henry VIII and Catherine of Aragon
- **C** Henry VIII and Jane Seymour
- **D** Henry VIII and Anne Boleyn

11 In 1948 Aneurin (Nye) Bevan led the establishment of the National Health Service (NHS). What was his role at the time?

- **A** Minister for Health
- **B** Deputy Prime Minister
- **C** Home Secretary
- **D** Minister for Social Security

12 What was the main source of employment in the UK before the Industrial Revolution?

- **A** Agriculture
- **B** The wool trade
- **C** Financial services
- **D** Canal building

13 Which of the following statements is correct?

- **A** The jet engine and radar were developed in Britain in the 1930s.
- **B** Information was first successfully transferred via the internet in the 1950s.

14 Is the statement below TRUE or FALSE?
By around AD 600, Anglo-Saxon kingdoms were established in Britain.

- **A** True
- **B** False

15 In 1649, England was declared a republic. What was it called?

- **A** The Commonwealth
- **B** The People's Republic
- **C** Cromwell's Republic
- **D** Great Britain

16 Which TWO of the following were members of the Royal Society?

- **A** Sir Christopher Wren
- **B** Samuel Pepys
- **C** Sir Edmond Halley
- **D** Sir Isaac Newton

17 Is it acceptable in the UK to treat people worse because of their sexual orientation?

- **A** Yes, if their sexual orientation is forbidden by religion
- **B** No, it is never acceptable to treat people worse because of their sexual orientation

18 Queen Elizabeth II is the head of state for which TWO of the following?

- **A** The United Kingdom
- **B** The European Union
- **C** Iceland
- **D** Many Commonwealth countries

19 Is the statement below TRUE or FALSE?
Sir Robert Walpole was Prime Minister from 1700 to 1730.

- **A** True
- **B** False

20 A snack made from flour, dried fruits and spices and served either hot or cold is which of the following?

- **A** A Scottish bun
- **B** An English muffin
- **C** An Irish pie
- **D** A Welsh cake

21 What is the name of the famous horse-race held near Liverpool?

A Grand Chase

B Grand Derby

C Steeplechase

D Grand National

22 NATO is a group of North American and European countries which have agreed to do which TWO of the following?

A Promote peace between member countries

B Promote traditional culture

C To protect each other when under attack

D To allow the free movement of people across borders

23 Is the statement below TRUE or FALSE?
Commercial expansion and prosperity in the 18th century were sustained in part by the booming slave trade.

A True

B False

24 Is the statement below TRUE or FALSE?
You have to be 16 or over to buy a drink in a public house (pub) or nightclub.

A True

B False

ANSWERS: PRACTICE TEST 4

			Study material reference
1	A	True	p17–8
2	B	Yes, but only in Scotland	p130
3	B	False	p86
4	B	Diktat	p124–5
5	B	False	p120
6	B	It kept its own educational system	p34
7	A	A dog's owner is responsible for keeping the animal under control and cleaning up after it in public places.	p94
8	A	True	p36
9	C	*Moby Dick*	p86
10	D	Henry VIII and Anne Boleyn	p22–4
11	A	Minister for Health	p52–3
12	A	Agriculture	p35–7
13	B	The jet engine and radar were developed in Britain in the 1930s.	p56–7
14	A	True	p13–5
15	A	The Commonwealth	p28–30
16	C	Sir Edmond Halley	p30
	D	Sir Isaac Newton	
17	B	No, it is never acceptable to treat people worse because of their sexual orientation	p140
18	A	The United Kingdom	p107–9
	D	Many Commonwealth countries	
19	B	False	p34
20	D	A Welsh cake	p90
21	D	Grand National	p77
22	A	Promote peace between member countries	p125
	C	To protect each other when under attack	
23	A	True	p37–8
24	B	False	p93

PRACTICE TEST 5

1 Is the statement below TRUE or FALSE?
The police do not need to protect and help people who are not UK citizens.

A True

B False

2 Is the statement below TRUE or FALSE?
The Channel Islands and the Isle of Man are part of the UK.

A True

B False

3 Is the statement below TRUE or FALSE?
The Puritans agreed with the religious reforms of the Church of England introduced by Charles I.

A True

B False

4 Which Catherine was executed after being accused of taking lovers by Henry VIII?

A Parr

B Boleyn

C Of Aragon

D Howard

5 Someone wishing to stand as a candidate for MP would need to be how old?

A 16

B 18

C 21

D There is no minimum age limit

6 Sir Anthony Van Dyck was famous as which of the following?

- **A** Actor
- **B** Painter
- **C** Sculptor
- **D** Composer

7 Which of the following takes place on 14 February every year?

- **A** St Christopher's Day
- **B** St George's Day
- **C** St Valentine's Day
- **D** All Saints Day

8 Which of the following statements is correct?

- **A** Chequers is the Prime Minister's country house.
- **B** Chequers is the Prime Minister's house in London.

9 Where did Florence Nightingale establish the Nightingale School for Nurses in 1860?

- **A** St Thomas' Hospital, London
- **B** Addenbrooke's Hospital, Cambridge
- **C** St James's University Hospital, Leeds
- **D** Prince Philip Hospital, Llanelli

10 What are small Scottish farms also known as?

- **A** Crofts
- **B** Bothies
- **C** Hamlets
- **D** Homesteads

11 Ian McEwan, Hilary Mantel and Julian Barnes have all won which literary prize?

- **A** The Turner Prize
- **B** The Man Booker Prize
- **C** The Nobel Prize in Literature
- **D** The Mercury Prize

12 For much of the Stone Age, Britain was connected to the continent by what?

- **A** A bridge
- **B** A land bridge
- **C** A glacier
- **D** A tunnel

13 Which of the following statements is correct?

- **A** Pantomimes are usually based on fairy stories.
- **B** Pantomimes are usually based on famous events from history.

14 In what way was Elizabeth I skilled at managing Parliament?

- **A** She established a balance between Catholics and Protestants by not persecuting either group
- **B** She reduced the power of Parliament so her wishes had more significance

15 The National Assembly makes laws for Wales in 20 areas. It does NOT make laws in which of the following areas?

- **A** Housing
- **B** Economic policy
- **C** Education and training
- **D** Health and social services

16 Why did the United States enter the Second World War in December 1941?

A The Japanese bombed its naval base at Pearl Harbor

B The Japanese bombed the US city of Seattle

C The Japanese arrested US civilians living in Japan

D The Japanese invaded the US state of Florida

17 Is the statement below TRUE or FALSE?
In the Middle Ages, England's system of 'common law' was established by referring to previous decisions and tradition.

A True

B False

18 Who became Prime Minister in May 2010?

A David Cameron

B Nick Clegg

C Ed Miliband

D Nigel Farage

19 Which Hindu and Sikh festival is normally celebrated in October or November every year?

A Diwali

B Vaisakhi

C Eid ul Adha

D Hannukah

20 Is the statement below TRUE or FALSE?
The small claims procedure is an informal way for people to settle minor disputes.

A True

B False

21 What event is commemorated on 5 November every year?

- **A** England's World Cup victory of 1966
- **B** The end of the First World War
- **C** A plot to blow up the Houses of Parliament
- **D** The Queen's birthday

22 What is Ridley Scott famous for?

- **A** Directing films
- **B** Theatre production
- **C** Conducting orchestras
- **D** Singing as an operatic tenor

23 Is the statement below TRUE or FALSE?
The UK is a parliamentary democracy.

- **A** True
- **B** False

24 Which of the following statements is correct?

- **A** Murder, assault and theft are crimes.
- **B** Murder, assault and theft are examples of civil disputes.

ANSWERS: PRACTICE TEST 5

			Study material reference
1	B	False	p127–8
2	B	False	p8
3	B	False	p28
4	D	Howard	p23
5	B	18	p114
6	B	Painter	p82–3
7	C	St Valentine's Day	p72
8	A	Chequers is the Prime Minister's country house.	p113
9	A	St Thomas' Hospital, London	p43
10	A	Crofts	p34–5
11	B	The Man Booker Prize	p85
12	B	A land bridge	p12–3
13	A	Pantomimes are usually based on fairy stories.	p81–2
14	A	She established a balance between Catholics and Protestants by not persecuting either group	p24–5
15	B	Economic policy	p116–7
16	A	The Japanese bombed its naval base at Pearl Harbor	p48–51
17	A	True	p18–19
18	A	David Cameron	p60
19	A	Diwali	p70–1
20	A	True	p133
21	C	A plot to blow up the Houses of Parliament	p72
22	A	Directing films	p90–1
23	A	True	p110
24	A	Murder, assault and theft are crimes.	p126–7

PRACTICE TEST 6

1 Which period of British history saw the emergence of a national culture and identity?

- **A** The Bronze Age
- **B** The Middle Ages
- **C** The Victorian period
- **D** The Tudor period

2 What is the capital city of the UK?

- **A** Birmingham
- **B** Liverpool
- **C** London
- **D** Sheffield

3 Is the statement below TRUE or FALSE?
Sir Steve Redgrave was the first man in the world to run a mile in under four minutes.

- **A** True
- **B** False

4 How many people emigrated from the UK between 1853 and 1913?

- **A** 100,000
- **B** 13 million
- **C** 500 million
- **D** 2 million

5 Which of the following statements is correct?

- **A** The declaration of rights read at the coronation of William and Mary meant the monarch could no longer raise taxes or administer justice.
- **B** The declaration of rights read at the coronation of William and Mary meant the monarch had absolute power to rule without the interference of Parliament.

6 Is the statement below TRUE or FALSE?
Sir Ian Botham captained the England rugby team.

- **A** True
- **B** False

7 Where did the Boer War take place?

- **A** South Africa
- **B** France
- **C** England
- **D** Turkey

8 Richard Arkwright used steam engines to do what?

- **A** Pull carriages
- **B** Power machinery
- **C** Create electricity
- **D** Make wigs

9 Henry VIII took which title in relation to Ireland?

- **A** Head
- **B** King
- **C** Lieutenant
- **D** Commander

10 Which of the following statements is correct?

- **A** During the 16th century the Scottish Parliament welcomed the authority of the Pope and Roman Catholic religious services became commonplace.
- **B** During the 16th century the Scottish Parliament abolished the authority of the Pope and Roman Catholic religious services became illegal.

11 Which of the following statements is correct?

- **A** A Magistrates' Court deals with only the most serious criminal cases.
- **B** A Magistrates' Court deals with minor criminal offences.

12 Eid al-Fitr celebrates the end of Ramadan. For how long before do Muslims fast?

- **A** Five days
- **B** Two weeks
- **C** One month
- **D** Twenty–one days

13 The National Eisteddfod is a major cultural festival which takes place in which country?

- **A** England
- **B** Scotland
- **C** Wales
- **D** Northern Ireland

14 Is the statement below TRUE or FALSE?
The threat of Viking attack caused the peoples in the north to unite, and the term Scotland was used to describe that country.

- **A** True
- **B** False

15 The British equivalent of the Oscars is hosted by BAFTA. For what do these initials stand?

- **A** British Association of Film and Technical Appliances
- **B** British Academy of Film and Theatre Awards
- **C** British Academy of Film and Television Arts
- **D** British Awards for Film and Television Actors

16 What information must always be entered on an electoral registration form?

- **A** Only the names of adult men resident at the address
- **B** The names of everyone at the address
- **C** The names of all eligible voters who live at the address
- **D** Only the names of adult women resident at the address

17 Who is the ceremonial head of the Commonwealth?

- **A** The Prime Minister
- **B** The President of the USA
- **C** The Queen
- **D** The Prince of Wales

18 The French Wars ended in 1815 when Napoleon was defeated by the Duke of Wellington at which battle?

- **A** Battle of Waterloo
- **B** Battle of Trafalgar
- **C** Battle of Ostend
- **D** Battle of Naseby

19 Which Anglo-Saxon poem tells of its hero's battles against monsters?

- **A** *Beowulf*
- **B** *The Fight at Finnsburh*
- **C** *Waldere*
- **D** *Deor*

20 Which of the following statements is correct?

- **A** The UK experienced high levels of employment during the Great Depression of the 1930s.
- **B** During the Great Depression of the 1930s parts of the UK experienced mass unemployment.

21 To apply to become a permanent resident or citizen of the UK you will need to be able to do which TWO of the following?

- **A** Speak and read English
- **B** Speak Welsh
- **C** Have a good understanding of life in the UK
- **D** Speak more than one language

22 Which of the following is a famous British film?

- **A** *Passport to Paddington*
- **B** *Passport to Portsmouth*
- **C** *Passport to Panama*
- **D** *Passport to Pimlico*

23 In a Crown Court, who decides what the penalty will be, in the case of a 'guilty' verdict?

- **A** A solicitor
- **B** The judge
- **C** The jury
- **D** A police officer

24 Every MP represents which of the following?

- **A** A constituency
- **B** A county
- **C** A city
- **D** Just the people who voted for them

ANSWERS: PRACTICE TEST 6

			Study material reference
1	B	The Middle Ages	p19–21
2	C	London	p63
3	B	False	p74–5
4	B	13 million	p41
5	A	The declaration of rights read at the coronation of William and Mary meant the monarch could no longer raise taxes or administer justice.	p33
6	B	False	p74–5
7	A	South Africa	p45
8	B	Power machinery	p36
9	B	King	p27
10	B	During the 16th century the Scottish Parliament abolished the authority of the Pope and Roman Catholic religious services became illegal.	p25
11	B	A Magistrates' Court deals with minor criminal offences.	p130
12	C	One month	p70–1
13	C	Wales	p79–81
14	A	True	p15
15	C	British Academy of Film and Television Arts	p90–1
16	C	The names of all eligible voters who live at the address	p120–1
17	C	The Queen	p123
18	A	Battle of Waterloo	p38–9
19	A	*Beowulf*	p86–8
20	B	During the Great Depression of the 1930s parts of the UK experienced mass unemployment.	p48
21	A	Speak and read English	p3–4
	C	Have a good understanding of life in the UK	
22	D	*Passport to Pimlico*	p90–1
23	B	The judge	p130
24	A	A constituency	p110

PRACTICE TEST 7

1 Who were the Huguenots?

- **A** Roman Catholics
- **B** French Catholics
- **C** Dutch Protestants
- **D** French Protestants

2 Which of the following statements is correct?

- **A** Employment opportunities for women are much greater than they were in the past.
- **B** Men now work in less varied jobs than they did in the past.

3 Who wrote the poem *The Tyger*?

- **A** William Wordsworth
- **B** William Blake
- **C** William Shakespeare
- **D** William Wallace

4 Which of the following statements is correct?

- **A** Robert Burns wrote only in Scots language.
- **B** Robert Burns wrote in Scots, English and a combination of both.

5 Is the statement below TRUE or FALSE?
The Prime Minister has had the power to nominate life peers since 1958.

- **A** True
- **B** False

6 Which of these statements is correct?

- **A** All the national saints' days are celebrated but only in Scotland and Northern Ireland are they official holidays.
- **B** All the national saints' days are celebrated but only in England and Wales are they official holidays.

7 Is it possible for parents or other community groups to open a free school?

- **A** Yes, in any part of the UK
- **B** Yes, but only in England

8 Which of the following will help you get along with your neighbours?

- **A** Only putting rubbish and recycling out on collection days
- **B** Having an untidy garden
- **C** Making lots of noise, especially late at night
- **D** Only introducing yourself to them after a year

9 Is the statement below TRUE or FALSE?
Cricket is the UK's most popular sport.

- **A** True
- **B** False

10 Which country was the composer George Frederick Handel born in?

- **A** England
- **B** America
- **C** Russia
- **D** Germany

11 Is the statement below TRUE or FALSE?
There has been a Welsh Assembly and a Scottish Parliament since 1999.

A True

B False

12 Is the statement below TRUE or FALSE?
France was the first country to industrialise on a large scale.

A True

B False

13 Which of these reasons best explains why town planning laws were tightened in the early 20th century?

A To protect the countryside

B To stop skyscrapers being built

C To allow for the building of new churches

D To prevent the further development of slums

14 Is the statement below TRUE or FALSE?
Thanks to its position as the world's leading industrial nation during the 1800s, Britain was responsible for producing half of the world's coal, iron and cotton cloth.

A True

B False

15 How often is Prime Minister's Questions held?

A Every day

B Every day whilst Parliament is in session

C Every week

D Every week whilst Parliament is in session

16 Which of the following statements is correct?

- **A** People in the UK are living longer than ever before.
- **B** The average lifespan for UK residents is steadily decreasing.

17 The Royal Society was formed to promote what?

- **A** Astrology
- **B** Natural knowledge
- **C** Art
- **D** Music

18 Who is the head of state?

- **A** The President
- **B** The Prime Minister
- **C** Prince Philip
- **D** The Queen

19 Which TWO events happened to the church in England following the restoration of Charles II?

- **A** The Church of England was restored as the official church
- **B** The Puritans and Roman Catholics were kept out of power
- **C** The Puritans grew in strength and number
- **D** The Church of England was suppressed

20 What is it traditional to do on 1 April in the UK?

- **A** Play musical instruments in the street
- **B** Play jokes on each other
- **C** Hunt for eggs
- **D** Make pancakes

21 Is the statement below TRUE or FALSE?
You must always tell a canvasser how you intend to vote.

- **A** True
- **B** False

22 Which of the following statements is correct?

- **A** Margaret Thatcher was the UK's first female Prime Minister.
- **B** Margaret Thatcher was the UK's second female Prime Minister.

23 Which of the following statements is correct?

- **A** Thomas Chippendale was an 18th century designer of furniture.
- **B** Sir Terence Conran was a 18th century designer of furniture.

24 John Petts was a Welshman famous in which TWO of these areas of art?

- **A** Stained glass
- **B** Water colours
- **C** Engraving
- **D** Paintings of horses

ANSWERS: PRACTICE TEST 7

			Study material reference
1	D	French Protestants	p34
2	A	Employment opportunities for women are much greater than they were in the past.	p65–6
3	B	William Blake	p86–88
4	B	Robert Burns wrote in Scots, English and a combination of both.	p35
5	A	True	p111
6	A	All the national saints' days are celebrated but only in Scotland and Northern Ireland are they official holidays.	p67–8
7	B	Yes, but only in England	p142–3
8	A	Only putting rubbish and recycling out on collection days	p141
9	B	False	p76
10	D	Germany	p79–81
11	A	True	p115
12	B	False	p35–7
13	D	To prevent the further development of slums	p46–7
14	A	True	p41–2
15	D	Every week whilst Parliament is in session	p114
16	A	People in the UK are living longer than ever before.	p65
17	B	Natural knowledge	p30
18	D	The Queen	p107–9
19	A	The Church of England was restored as the official church	p30
	B	The Puritans and Roman Catholics were kept out of power	
20	B	Play jokes on each other	p72
21	B	False	p143
22	A	Margaret Thatcher was the UK's first female Prime Minister.	p58
23	A	Thomas Chippendale was an 18th century designer of furniture.	p85
24	A	Stained glass	p83
	C	Engraving	

PRACTICE TEST 8

1 The Chancellor of the Exchequer is responsible for which area of government policy?

- **A** Health
- **B** Defence
- **C** The economy
- **D** Immigration

2 The Scottish Parliament can make laws in which of the following areas?

- **A** Health
- **B** Taxation
- **C** Civil and criminal law
- **D** All of the above

3 The UK is a permanent member of the UN Security Council. How many permanent members does the Security Council have?

- **A** 5
- **B** 15
- **C** 27
- **D** 190

4 The Industrial Revolution saw the rapid growth of which of the following in the 18th and 19th centuries?

- **A** Agriculture
- **B** Democracy
- **C** Population
- **D** Industry

5 On his escape from the Battle of Worcester, Charles II famously hid inside what?

- **A** A forest
- **B** An oak tree
- **C** A cellar
- **D** None of the above

6 The heptathlon comprises how many different track and field events?

- **A** 5
- **B** 6
- **C** 7
- **D** 8

7 Which statement describes 'party politics' during the reign of William and Mary?

- **A** There were two main groups, the Liberals and the Conservatives.
- **B** There were two main groups, the Tories and the Whigs.

8 Which of the following is NOT the job of the police?

- **A** To prosecute someone for debt
- **B** To keep the peace
- **C** To prevent and detect crime
- **D** To protect life and property

9 After the Glorious Revolution, Parliament was still some way from being a democracy. Why?

- **A** Only bishops were able to vote
- **B** Only men who owned property of a certain value could vote
- **C** Only women were allowed to vote
- **D** Parliament took control of who could be monarch

10 Is the statement below TRUE or FALSE?
All Acts of Parliament are made in the name of the Prime Minister.

- **A** True
- **B** False

11 Coinage in the United Kingdom consists of 1p, 2p, 5p, 10p, 20p, 50p, £1 and which other coin?

- **A** 25p
- **B** £8
- **C** £3
- **D** £2

12 Which of the following is a line from one of Churchill's famous speeches?

- **A** I have a dream
- **B** The lady's not for turning
- **C** The only thing we have to fear is fear itself
- **D** I have nothing to offer but blood, toil, tears and sweat

13 Which TWO of the following are freedoms offered to citizens and permanent residents of the UK?

- **A** Freedom of speech
- **B** Half day off work on Friday
- **C** A right to take part in the election of a government
- **D** Free heating for all

14 In which city is the Scottish Parliament based?

- **A** Sheffield
- **B** Edinburgh
- **C** Glasgow
- **D** Cardiff

15 Which Scottish poet wrote *The Bruce* about the Battle of Bannockburn?

- **A** Robert Burns
- **B** John Barbour
- **C** Geoffrey Chaucer
- **D** John Milton

16 Which of the following statements is correct?

- **A** During Queen Victoria's reign, the middle classes became increasingly significant.
- **B** During Queen Victoria's reign, the size and influence of the British middle class shrank.

17 Rudyard Kipling was awarded which major prize in 1907?

- **A** The Man Booker Prize
- **B** The Pulitzer Prize
- **C** The Nobel Prize in Literature
- **D** The Somerset Maugham Award

18 The Rugby Union Six Nations Championship comprises England, Wales, Scotland and Ireland and which TWO of the following teams?

- **A** South Africa
- **B** Italy
- **C** France
- **D** Argentina

19 Who wrote the poem *She Walks in Beauty*?

- **A** Sir John Betjeman
- **B** Sir Walter de la Mare
- **C** Elizabeth Browning
- **D** Lord Byron

20 Is the statement below TRUE or FALSE?
The Education Act of 1944 is often called The Butler Act and introduced free secondary education in England and Wales.

A True

B False

21 What are members of the Northern Ireland Assembly known as?

A MPs

B MNIPs

C MLAs

D MEPs

22 Which of these films was directed by David Lean?

A *Women in Love*

B *Four Weddings and a Funeral*

C *The Killing Fields*

D *Brief Encounter*

23 What is the common name for the Yeoman Warders at the Tower of London?

A Pikestaff

B Queen's Men

C Crown Guards

D Beefeaters

24 Is the statement below TRUE or FALSE?
A mayor is always elected.

A True

B False

ANSWERS: PRACTICE TEST 8

			Study material reference
1	C	The economy	p113–4
2	A	Health	p118
3	A	5	p125
4	D	Industry	p35–7
5	B	An oak tree	p28–30
6	C	7	p74–5
7	B	There were two main groups, the Tories and the Whigs.	p33
8	A	To prosecute someone for debt	p127–8
9	B	Only men who owned property of a certain value could vote	p33
10	B	False	p107–9
11	D	£2	p64
12	D	I have nothing to offer but blood, toil, tears and sweat	p50
13	A	Freedom of speech	p2–3
	C	A right to take part in the election of a government	
14	B	Edinburgh	p118
15	B	John Barbour	p19–21
16	A	During Queen Victoria's reign, the middle classes became increasingly significant.	p41
17	C	The Nobel Prize in Literature	p45
18	B	Italy	p77
	C	France	
19	D	Lord Byron	p86–8
20	A	True	p54
21	C	MLAs	p122–3
22	D	*Brief Encounter*	p91
23	D	Beefeaters	p95–103
24	B	False	p115

PRACTICE TEST 9

1 Which of the following is a famous television series?

- **A** *Monty Python's Flying Clowns*
- **B** *Monty Python's Flying Snakes*
- **C** *Monty Python's Flying Fanatics*
- **D** *Monty Python's Flying Circus*

2 What was inscribed on some Iron Age coins?

- **A** Dates
- **B** Values
- **C** Names of Iron Age kings
- **D** Names of Iron Age settlements

3 During the 16th century which TWO factors predominantly led to a bloody rebellion by the Irish chieftains?

- **A** Extreme poverty and famine
- **B** The imposing of English laws on land inheritance
- **C** High taxes on landowners
- **D** The imposing of Protestantism

4 The Assembly Booking Service assists people who wish to book a guided tour of the Senedd or which of the following?

- **A** Book a seat in the public gallery
- **B** Buy a ticket to see the Welsh National Opera
- **C** Buy a ticket to view a public debate
- **D** Buy a ticket to Prime Minister's Questions

5 Which one of these statements is correct?

- **A** Every person in the UK requires a television licence.
- **B** Every household in the UK which has a television or device which receives television programmes must have a television licence.

6 Which TWO of these countries did poet and author Rudyard Kipling spend time living in?

- **A** India
- **B** Japan
- **C** Fiji
- **D** USA

7 Is the statement below TRUE or FALSE?
The Canterbury Tales *was one of the first books to be printed by William Caxton.*

- **A** True
- **B** False

8 Acts of Parliament in 1870 and 1882 awarded which right to women?

- **A** The right to bear arms
- **B** The right to work
- **C** The right to attend university
- **D** The right to keep their own earnings and property after marriage

9 During the early 1970s, Britain admitted 28,000 people of Indian origin who had been forced to leave where?

- **A** The West Indies
- **B** South Africa
- **C** China
- **D** Uganda

10 To go into a betting shop or casino, you have to be what age?

- **A** 15
- **B** 16
- **C** 17
- **D** 18

11 Which of these is NOT a Gilbert and Sullivan comic opera?

- **A** *The Pirates of Penzance*
- **B** *The Mikado*
- **C** *A Midsummer Night's Dream*
- **D** *HMS Pinafore*

12 William of Normandy invaded England in 1066. Where is Normandy?

- **A** Southern Scotland
- **B** Denmark
- **C** Northern France
- **D** Norway

13 Causing trouble whilst drinking in public can result in which TWO of the following from the police?

- **A** An award
- **B** Arrest
- **C** A fine
- **D** Praise

14 The English Parliament during the reign of Charles I contained many Puritans. What did the Puritans believe in?

- **A** Simple and strict religious doctrine and worship
- **B** Roman Catholic religious doctrine and worship
- **C** The power of the nobility to control Parliament
- **D** None of the above

15 What happens at a polling station or polling place?

- **A** The census is collected
- **B** People vote in elections
- **C** Taxes are collected
- **D** People take their driving test

16 Which of the following statements is correct?

- **A** Big Ben refers to the great bell of the clock at the Houses of Parliament.
- **B** *Big Ben* is a novel written by Sir Kingsley Amis.

17 Around which structure in London is the Remembrance Day service usually held?

- **A** The statue of Eros in Piccadilly Circus
- **B** Nelson's Column in Trafalgar Square
- **C** The London Eye
- **D** The Cenotaph in Whitehall

18 Which of the following statements is correct?

- **A** Dogs in public places must wear a muzzle.
- **B** Dogs in public places must wear a collar showing the owner's name and address.
- **C** Cats in public places must wear a collar.
- **D** All dog owners must have a licence to keep their pets.

19 Which one of the following is NOT one of the purposes of the National Citizen Service programme?

- **A** To give young people a chance to develop skills
- **B** To train young people for the army
- **C** To give 16- and 17-year-olds a chance to volunteer
- **D** To give young people a chance to enjoy outdoor activities

20 Which king annexed Wales to the Crown of England with the Statute of Rhuddlan?

- **A** Charles I
- **B** Harold
- **C** Henry VIII
- **D** Edward I

21 Which of the following statements is correct?

- **A** Colonists in North America were well educated and interested in ideas of liberty.
- **B** Colonists in North America were poorly educated and uninterested in politics.

22 Where did Mary Stuart spend most of her childhood?

- **A** France
- **B** Germany
- **C** Spain
- **D** England

23 The UK has what kind of monarchy?

- **A** Democratic
- **B** Constitutional
- **C** Provisional
- **D** Absolute

24 Is the statement below TRUE or FALSE?
The candidate who wins the most votes is elected MP for the constituency.

- **A** True
- **B** False

ANSWERS: PRACTICE TEST 9

			Study material reference
1	D	*Monty Python's Flying Circus*	p91–2
2	C	Names of Iron Age kings	p12–3
3	B	The imposing of English laws on land inheritance	p22–4
	D	The imposing of Protestantism	
4	A	Book a seat in the public gallery	p122–3
5	B	Every household in the UK which has a television or device which receives television programmes must have a television licence.	p92–3
6	A	India	p45
	D	USA	
7	A	True	p19–21
8	D	The right to keep their own earnings and property after marriage	p43–4
9	D	Uganda	p55
10	D	18	p93–4
11	C	*A Midsummer Night's Dream*	p81–2
12	C	Northern France	p15–6
13	B	Arrest	p126–7
	C	A fine	
14	A	Simple and strict religious doctrine and worship	p28
15	B	People vote in elections	p121
16	A	Big Ben refers to the great bell of the clock at the Houses of Parliament.	p95–103
17	D	The Cenotaph in Whitehall	p72
18	B	Dogs in public places must wear a collar showing the owner's name and address.	p94
19	B	To train young people for the army	p144–6
20	D	Edward I	p17
21	A	Colonists in North America were well educated and interested in ideas of liberty.	p38
22	A	France	p25
23	B	Constitutional	p107
24	A	True	p112

PRACTICE TEST 10

1 **The first farmers probably came to Britain from where?**

- **A** Norway
- **B** South-east Europe
- **C** North America
- **D** North-west Europe

2 **Which of the following statements is correct?**

- **A** Britain has never hosted the Olympic Games.
- **B** Britain hosted the Olympic Games in 1908, 1948 and 2012.

3 **How many people make up a Scottish jury?**

- **A** 10
- **B** 12
- **C** 15
- **D** 20

4 **What is a Yorkshire pudding?**

- **A** A caramel-flavoured dessert
- **B** Meat and potato in a pastry
- **C** Batter cooked in the oven
- **D** Apple and pears with custard

5 **Is the statement below TRUE or FALSE?**
Charles II marched into England with a Scottish army to reclaim his throne.

- **A** True
- **B** False

6 Is the statement below TRUE or FALSE?
A jump jet capable of taking off and landing vertically was developed in the UK, and was called the Falcon.

- **A** True
- **B** False

7 Is the statement below TRUE or FALSE?
The Domesday Book no longer exists. It was destroyed at the end of the Norman Conquest.

- **A** True
- **B** False

8 What are MEPs?

- **A** Members of the English Parliament
- **B** Members of the European Parliament
- **C** Modern English parliamentarians
- **D** Modern European parliamentarians

9 Is the statement below TRUE or FALSE?
The MacDonald clan of Glencoe were massacred.

- **A** True
- **B** False

10 Is the statement below TRUE or FALSE?
The Northern Ireland Assembly was elected in 1999, suspended in 2002 and reinstated again in 2007.

- **A** True
- **B** False

11 Is the statement below TRUE or FALSE?
At the beginning of the Middle Ages, England ruled Ireland.

- **A** True
- **B** False

12 Which of the following statements is correct?

- **A** The cabinet's decisions often have to be debated or approved by Parliament.
- **B** The cabinet's decisions must always be debated or approved by Parliament.

13 Who became queen after the death of Edward VI?

- **A** His half-sister Mary
- **B** His wife Mary
- **C** His cousin Mary
- **D** Mary, Queen of Scots

14 Which TWO of the following statements are correct?

- **A** The Romans built roads, public buildings and created a structure of law.
- **B** The Romans unified the whole of the British Isles.
- **C** The Roman army faced no resistance during the invasions.
- **D** The Romans introduced new plants and animals to Britain.

15 What do you accept and agree to when you become a permanent resident of the UK?

- **A** Catholic beliefs and values
- **B** The right to be tried for crimes in your country of origin
- **C** Traditions of the UK
- **D** Protestant beliefs and values

16 Is the statement below TRUE or FALSE?
The Home Office selects who becomes a Police and Crime Commissioner (PCC).

- **A** True
- **B** False

17 Is the following statement TRUE or FALSE?
Queen Victoria's reign ended in 1952.

- **A** True
- **B** False

18 How is the electoral register updated?

- **A** Eligible voters must phone their local councillor
- **B** Every household receives a registration form, which must be completed and returned
- **C** Every household must request a registration form
- **D** Every household receives a phone call to enquire about eligible voters

19 Is the statement below TRUE or FALSE?
The Welsh Assembly has no power to make laws, but considerable control over public services.

- **A** True
- **B** False

20 The Archbishop of Canterbury can most accurately be described as what?

- **A** The spiritual leader of the Church of England
- **B** The political leader of the Church of England
- **C** The administrative leader of the Church of England
- **D** The financial leader of the Church of England

21 What were *The Canterbury Tales*?

- **A** A book of Christian doctrine
- **B** A series of poems
- **C** A Royal Charter
- **D** A story about Canterbury Cathedral

22 Which of the following statements is correct?

- **A** The House of Commons may overrule the House of Lords.
- **B** The House of Commons may never overrule the House of Lords.

23 Which of the following statements is correct?

- **A** The UK's constitution is unwritten but includes laws and conventions.
- **B** The UK's constitution is a single document which includes laws and conventions.

24 Which TWO of the following have the right to vote?

- **A** Adults who have been granted an indefinite right to remain in the UK
- **B** Adults who were born in the UK
- **C** Adults who have been given a visa to study in the UK
- **D** Adults who are naturalised citizens of the UK

ANSWERS: PRACTICE TEST 10

			Study material reference
1	B	South-east Europe	p12–3
2	B	Britain hosted the Olympic Games in 1908, 1948 and 2012.	p74
3	C	15	p130
4	C	Batter cooked in the oven	p90
5	A	True	p28–30
6	B	False	p56–7
7	B	False	p15–6
8	B	Members of the European Parliament	p112
9	A	True	p31–2
10	A	True	p59
11	B	False	p17
12	A	The cabinet's decisions often have to be debated or approved by Parliament.	p113–4
13	A	His half-sister Mary	p22–4
14	A	The Romans built roads, public buildings and created a structure of law.	p13
	D	The Romans introduced new plants and animals to Britain.	
15	C	Traditions of the UK	p2–3
16	B	False	p127–8
17	B	False	p41
18	B	Every household receives a registration form, which must be completed and returned	p120–1
19	B	False	p59
20	A	The spiritual leader of the Church of England	p67
21	B	A series of poems	p19–21
22	A	The House of Commons may overrule the House of Lords.	p111
23	A	The UK's constitution is unwritten but includes laws and conventions.	p107
24	B	Adults who were born in the UK	p120
	D	Adults who are naturalised citizens of the UK	

PRACTICE TEST 11

1 **Where would the Children's Hearings System deal with cases of children or young people accused of an offence?**

A Northern Ireland

B Wales

C England

D Scotland

2 **Areas of protected countryside that everyone can visit and where people live, work and look after the landscape are called which of the following?**

A Greenfield sites

B Country estates

C National parks

D Moorland

3 **Is the statement below TRUE or FALSE?**
In 55 BC, Julius Caesar led the Roman invasion of Britain.

A True

B False

4 **What was the Spanish Armada?**

A A fleet of Spanish ships

B A Spanish princess

C A treaty with Spain

D The Spanish Army

5 Is the statement below TRUE or FALSE?
Dame Judi Dench, Colin Firth and Sir Anthony Hopkins have all won Oscars.

- **A** True
- **B** False

6 The first people lived in Britain during which period?

- **A** Ancient times
- **B** The Jurassic period
- **C** The Bronze Age
- **D** The Stone Age

7 In which language was *The Canterbury Tales* written?

- **A** French
- **B** Welsh
- **C** Scottish Gaelic
- **D** English

8 In England, parliaments were called when the king needed to consult the nobles and for what other reason?

- **A** To lower taxes
- **B** To create new lords
- **C** To raise money
- **D** To call elections

9 Is the statement below TRUE or FALSE?
The UK is a parliamentary democracy.

- **A** True
- **B** False

10 Is the statement below TRUE or FALSE?
The first Union Flag was created in 1606.

- **A** True
- **B** False

11 At the beginning of the 19th century, which one of the following groups could vote?

- **A** All adults over the age of 18
- **B** All women who owned property
- **C** Property-owning men over the age of 21
- **D** Property-owning men over the age of 18

12 Lewis Hamilton is a leading figure in which sport?

- **A** Motor racing
- **B** Horse racing
- **C** Tennis
- **D** Squash

13 Charles II had no legitimate what?

- **A** Right to the throne
- **B** Children
- **C** Government
- **D** Wife

14 Where can *HMS Victory* be visited?

- **A** Southampton
- **B** Falmouth
- **C** Poole
- **D** Portsmouth

15 The Northern Ireland Assembly makes decisions in which TWO of the following areas?

- **A** Agriculture
- **B** Nuclear energy
- **C** Foreign policy
- **D** The environment

16 From which TWO places did the Vikings come from?

- **A** Belgium
- **B** France
- **C** Denmark
- **D** Norway

17 Which TWO facts are true of the individual voter registration system?

- **A** Registered voters remain on the register until a change in their personal details
- **B** Eligible voters complete their own voter registration forms
- **C** An individual registers his or her whole family to vote
- **D** The electoral register is fully updated each year

18 What did Iron Age people sometimes defend?

- **A** Hill forts
- **B** Castles
- **C** Long walls
- **D** None of the above

19 Which of the following statements is correct?

- **A** You should always introduce yourself to your neighbours when you move into a new house or flat.
- **B** You should never introduce yourself to your new neighbours, but should let them introduce themselves.

20 When did Parliament as we know it today begin to develop?

- **A** The Iron Age
- **B** The Stone Age
- **C** The Middle Ages
- **D** The Bronze Age

21 Which TWO actions can political parties undertake to gain support for their candidate?

- **A** Threatening people to make them vote a certain way
- **B** Handing out leaflets
- **C** Knocking on doors and talking to people about their candidate
- **D** Paying people to vote a certain way

22 In the 19th century the UK became a world centre for which of the following sectors or industries?

- **A** Financial services
- **B** Agriculture
- **C** Wine-making
- **D** Entertainment

23 Is the statement below TRUE or FALSE?
ISAF is building up the Afghan National Security Forces and helping to create a secure environment in which governance and development can be extended.

- **A** True
- **B** False

24 Which of the following is NOT usually the role of a PCSO?

- **A** Working with the public
- **B** Supporting police officers at crime scenes and major events
- **C** Patrolling the streets
- **D** Treating injured people

ANSWERS: PRACTICE TEST 11

			Study material reference
1	D	Scotland	p131
2	C	National parks	p94
3	A	True	p13
4	A	A fleet of Spanish ships	p25–6
5	A	True	p90–1
6	D	The Stone Age	p12–3
7	D	English	p19–21
8	C	To raise money	p18–9
9	A	True	p110
10	A	True	p40
11	C	Property-owning men over the age of 21	p106
12	A	Motor racing	p78
13	B	Children	p31
14	D	Portsmouth	p38–9
15	A	Agriculture	p118–19
	D	The environment	
16	C	Denmark	p15
	D	Norway	
17	A	Registered voters remain on the register until a change in their personal details	p120–1
	B	Eligible voters complete their own voter registration forms	
18	A	Hill forts	p12–3
19	A	You should always introduce yourself to your neighbours when you move into a new house or flat.	p141
20	C	The Middle Ages	p18–9
21	B	Handing out leaflets	p143
	C	Knocking on doors and talking to people about their candidate	
22	A	Financial services	p41–2
23	A	True	p59–60
24	D	Treating injured people	p127–8

PRACTICE TEST 12

1 **Who was William Shakespeare?**

- **A** A naval commander
- **B** A Scottish patriot
- **C** An English parliamentarian
- **D** A poet, actor and playwright

2 **Which of the following statements is correct?**

- **A** The leaders of the Easter Rising were executed under military law.
- **B** The leaders of the Easter Rising were transported to Australia.

3 **Charles I believed in, and tried to rule in line with, what principle?**

- **A** Democracy
- **B** Communism
- **C** Religious virtue
- **D** The Divine Right of Kings

4 **Who is the heir to the throne?**

- **A** Prince Philip
- **B** Prince Charles
- **C** The Prime Minister
- **D** Prince Harry

5 **Which of the following statements is correct?**

- **A** More than 190 countries belong to NATO.
- **B** More than 190 countries belong to the United Nations.

6 During the First World War the British fought against countries including Germany, the Ottoman Empire and the Austro–Hungarian Empire. What was this alliance known as?

- **A** The Middle Powers
- **B** The Central Powers
- **C** The Germanic Powers
- **D** The Autocratic Powers

7 Is the statement below TRUE or FALSE?
Breaking a Forced Marriage Protection Order can result in a prison sentence.

- **A** True
- **B** False

8 Which composer, born in 1874, wrote *The Planets*?

- **A** Gustav Holst
- **B** Ralph Vaughan Williams
- **C** Sir Edward Elgar
- **D** Benjamin Britten

9 When did the first farmers come to Britain?

- **A** 10,000 years ago
- **B** 3,000 years ago
- **C** 6,000 years ago
- **D** 8,000 years ago

10 Is the statement below TRUE or FALSE?
During the Industrial Revolution canals were built to link factories to cities, towns and ports, particularly in the middle and north of England.

- **A** True
- **B** False

11 Who could not get Parliament to agree to their religious and foreign policy views and tried to rule without Parliament?

A Charles I

B Elizabeth I

C Bloody Mary

D Henry VIII

12 In the UK it is acceptable to discriminate against people for which of the following?

A Age

B Religion or beliefs

C Pregnancy or maternity

D None of the above

13 During the reign of which king of England was the Domesday Book compiled?

A Harold

B William the Conqueror

C Kenneth MacAlpin

D Alfred the Great

14 Which TWO of the following deal with civil disputes?

A Sheriff Court

B Crown Court

C County Court

D Youth Court

15 Which of the following is a core value of the civil service?

A Laziness

B Party loyalty

C Integrity

D Bribery

16 A vehicle more than three years old must pass an MOT test every year. What does MOT stand for?

- **A** Maintenance of Transportation
- **B** Migrant Order for Transport
- **C** Motor-vehicle Optimisation Test
- **D** Ministry of Transport

17 Is the statement below TRUE or FALSE?
King Henry I was on the throne at the time of the Magna Carta.

- **A** True
- **B** False

18 Who was Kenneth MacAlpin?

- **A** A Danish king
- **B** An Anglo–Saxon king
- **C** A Scottish king
- **D** A Viking

19 In which country are Loch Lomond and the Trossachs National Park found?

- **A** Wales
- **B** England
- **C** Scotland
- **D** Northern Ireland

20 A poll card includes which TWO pieces of information?

- **A** The date of the election
- **B** Who you should vote for
- **C** Where the polling station or polling place is located
- **D** How much tax you should pay

21 West Germany, France, Luxembourg, the Netherlands and Italy formed the European Economic Community (EEC) in 1957 along with which other country?

- **A** Ireland
- **B** Belgium
- **C** Sweden
- **D** Albania

22 Which of the following statements is correct?

- **A** Eid al-Fitr takes place on 20 November.
- **B** The date when Eid al-Fitr takes place changes every year.

23 Is everyone's income taxed automatically?

- **A** No, some people must complete a self-assessment tax form and then pay any taxes they might owe
- **B** Yes, everyone automatically pays the correct amount through PAYE

24 Is the statement below TRUE or FALSE?
Equal treatment under law means that the law applies in the same way to everyone, as long as they were born in the UK.

- **A** True
- **B** False

ANSWERS: PRACTICE TEST 12

			Study material reference
1	D	A poet, actor and playwright	p26
2	A	The leaders of the Easter Rising were executed under military law.	p47–8
3	D	The Divine Right of Kings	p27–8
4	B	Prince Charles	p107–9
5	B	More than 190 countries belong to the United Nations.	p125
6	B	The Central Powers	p46–7
7	A	True	p137
8	A	Gustav Holst	p79–81
9	C	6,000 years ago	p12–3
10	A	True	p35–7
11	A	Charles I	p27–8
12	D	None of the above	p136
13	B	William the Conqueror	p15–6
14	A	Sheriff Court	p133
	C	County Court	
15	C	Integrity	p115
16	D	Ministry of Transport	p139
17	B	False	p18–9
18	C	A Scottish king	p15
19	C	Scotland	p95–103
20	A	The date of the election	p121
	C	Where the polling station or polling place is located	
21	B	Belgium	p58
22	B	The date when Eid al-Fitr takes place changes every year.	p70–1
23	A	No, some people must complete a self-assessment tax form and then pay any taxes they might owe	p137–8
24	B	False	p126–7

PRACTICE TEST 13

1 Which of the following statements is correct?

- **A** Trading hours for shops in the UK do not change on public holidays.
- **B** Trading hours for shops in the UK are generally reduced on public holidays.

2 How many members does a jury have in England?

- **A** 10
- **B** 12
- **C** 15
- **D** 20

3 Mary Stuart, the queen of Scotland, was often known by which other name?

- **A** Mary Tudor
- **B** Bloody Mary
- **C** Mary, Queen of the Highlands
- **D** Mary, Queen of Scots

4 Which famous composer was born in 1857 in Worcester, England and wrote the *Pomp and Circumstance Marches*?

- **A** Sir William Walton
- **B** George Frederick Handel
- **C** Henry Purcell
- **D** Sir Edward Elgar

5 Which of these statements about Roald Dahl is NOT true?

- **A** He began to publish books and short stories in the 1940s.
- **B** He served in the Royal Air Force during the Second World War
- **C** He had Norwegian parents
- **D** He served in the Royal Navy during the Second World War

6 Which of the following statements is correct?

- **A** In Scotland, serious offences are tried in a Sheriff Court.
- **B** Serious offences are tried in a Sheriff Court everywhere in the UK.

7 During 1940, German troops defeated allied forces whilst advancing through which country?

- **A** Russia
- **B** France
- **C** Greece
- **D** Argentina

8 In which TWO places are arrangements different for taking the Life in the UK Test?

- **A** Scotland
- **B** Ireland
- **C** Isle of Man
- **D** Channel Islands

9 Which of the following was a co-discoverer of insulin?

- **A** John Logie Baird
- **B** Sir Frank Whittle
- **C** John MacLeod
- **D** Sir Robert Watson–Watt

10 The first day of one notorious battle in 1916 resulted in 60,000 British casualties. What was this battle?

- **A** The Battle of the Somme
- **B** The Battle of the Bulge
- **C** The Battle of Agincourt
- **D** The Battle of the River Plate

11 Which of the following is NOT a principle guarded by the European Convention on Human Rights?

- **A** The prohibition of slavery and forced labour
- **B** Freedom of thought, conscience and religion
- **C** The right to happiness
- **D** The right to a fair trial

12 During which king's reign in 1665 was there a major outbreak of plague in London?

- **A** Charles II
- **B** James I
- **C** James II
- **D** Charles I

13 What were women campaigning for the right to vote known as?

- **A** Suffragettes
- **B** Votettes
- **C** Democrettes
- **D** Feminettes

14 In Scotland, the legal system developed differently from in England in that its laws were 'codified'. What is meant by codified?

- **A** Less complicated
- **B** Dictated by parliament
- **C** Written down
- **D** Based on tradition

15 Is the statement below TRUE or FALSE?
Charles I was interested in science. During his reign, the Royal Society was formed.

- **A** True
- **B** False

16 Which TWO of these careers did Winston Churchill follow before becoming a Conservative MP in 1900?

- **A** Teacher
- **B** Vicar
- **C** Journalist
- **D** Soldier

17 What did the missionaries teach the Anglo-Saxons?

- **A** About other cultures
- **B** About Christianity
- **C** About other languages
- **D** About trade

18 Which of the following statements is correct?

- **A** James I and Charles I were very skilled at negotiating with Parliament.
- **B** James I and Charles I believed in the 'Divine Right of Kings' and that they could rule without the approval of Parliament

19 Is the statement below TRUE or FALSE?
The symbol of the House of Lancaster was a red rose and the symbol of the House of York was a white rose.

- **A** True
- **B** False

20 Who wrote *Paradise Lost*?

- **A** William Shakespeare
- **B** Salman Rushdie
- **C** Rider Haggard
- **D** John Milton

21 The Festival of Lights is another name for which of the following?

- **A** Vaisakhi
- **B** Hannukah
- **C** Diwali
- **D** Eid ul Adha

22 Anyone who wishes to stand for public office must be at least what age?

- **A** 16
- **B** 18
- **C** 21
- **D** 25

23 The game of golf is traditionally thought to have originated in which country?

- **A** England
- **B** Spain
- **C** USA
- **D** Scotland

24 Is the statement below TRUE or FALSE?
The Good Friday Agreement is also known as the Belfast Agreement.

- **A** True
- **B** False

ANSWERS: PRACTICE TEST 13

			Study material reference
1	B	Trading hours for shops in the UK are generally reduced on public holidays.	p89
2	B	12	p130
3	D	Mary, Queen of Scots	p25
4	D	Sir Edward Elgar	p79–81
5	D	He served in the Royal Navy during the Second World War	p59
6	A	In Scotland, serious offences are tried in a Sheriff Court.	p130
7	B	France	p48–51
8	C	Isle of Man	p4
	D	Channel Islands	
9	C	John MacLeod	p56–7
10	A	The Battle of the Somme	p46–7
11	C	The right to happiness	p135–6
12	A	Charles II	p30
13	A	Suffragettes	p43–4
14	C	Written down	p18–9
15	B	False	p30
16	C	Journalist	p50
	D	Soldier	
17	B	About Christianity	p13–5
18	B	James I and Charles I believed in the 'Divine Right of Kings' and that they could rule without the approval of Parliament	p27–8
19	A	True	p21
20	D	John Milton	p86–8
21	C	Diwali	p70–1
22	B	18	p121–2
23	D	Scotland	p77
24	A	True	p118–9

PRACTICE TEST 14

1 Which of the following is NOT a benefit of volunteering?

- **A** Being able to add new experience to your CV
- **B** Getting paid
- **C** Having a chance to practise your English
- **D** Meeting new people

2 What did hereditary peers lose in 1999?

- **A** The right to own land
- **B** The automatic right to sit in the House of Lords
- **C** The right to elect other peers to the House of Lords
- **D** The right to speak in Parliament

3 Jane Seymour gave birth to the son Henry VIII wanted. What was his name?

- **A** Henry
- **B** Edmund
- **C** Edward
- **D** Richard

4 If you can't make it to a polling station to vote you can register for which of the following?

- **A** A postal ballot
- **B** An absentee ballot
- **C** An absentee vote
- **D** A virtual ballot

5 Is the sentence below TRUE or FALSE?
Al Qa'ida is the only terrorist threat to the UK.

- **A** True
- **B** False

6 Is this statement TRUE or FALSE?
During Queen Victoria's reign the French Empire became the largest empire the world has ever seen.

- **A** True
- **B** False

7 Who decides what should happen in legal disputes over contracts, property rights or employment rights?

- **A** The media
- **B** The police
- **C** The judiciary
- **D** The peers

8 During the 18th century, Britain fought a number of wars with which country?

- **A** India
- **B** South Africa
- **C** Spain
- **D** France

9 Which of the following statements is correct?

- **A** The National Assembly for Wales and the Welsh government are based in Edinburgh.
- **B** The National Assembly for Wales and the Welsh government are based in Cardiff.

10 Which of the following statements is correct?

A The Commonwealth is a group of countries which support each other and work together.

B The Commonwealth is a group of regions which together make up a federal republic.

11 Is the statement below TRUE or FALSE?
Mo Farah was the first person to sail around the world single-handed.

A True

B False

12 What sorts of stories were depicted in the stained glass windows of many cathedrals built in the Middle Ages?

A Stories about kings and coronations

B Stories about battles and victories

C Stories about the Bible and saints

D Stories about communities and farming

13 Is the statement below TRUE or FALSE?
St Columba became the first Archbishop of Canterbury.

A True

B False

14 Is the statement below TRUE or FALSE?
Sake Dean Mahomet was born in 1759 and grew up in the Bengal region of India.

A True

B False

15 May members of the House of Lords stand for public office?

A Yes, except as candidates for the House of Commons

B Yes, but only by first resigning from the House of Lords

16 Which organisation was founded in 1895 and now has over 61,000 volunteers helping to preserve important buildings, the countryside and the coastline?

- **A** The National Trust
- **B** The Countryside Alliance
- **C** Country Landowners Association
- **D** The National Gardens Scheme

17 Which of the following was the composer Ralph Vaughan Williams strongly influenced by?

- **A** Traditional German folk music
- **B** Traditional Scottish folk music
- **C** Traditional English folk music
- **D** Traditional Irish folk music

18 During the reign of Henry VII what happened to the power of the nobility in England?

- **A** It was reduced
- **B** It increased
- **C** It was abolished
- **D** It was absolute

19 Is the statement below TRUE or FALSE?
The Old Bailey is one of the world's most famous Magistrates' Courts.

- **A** True
- **B** False

20 During the 19th century, Britain and the East India Company gained control of large parts of which TWO countries?

- **A** The United States
- **B** Canada
- **C** India
- **D** Singapore

21 Is the statement below TRUE or FALSE?
The Hundred Years War between England and France lasted 99 years.

- **A** True
- **B** False

22 Which of the following statements is correct?

- **A** The UK population in 1801 was smaller than the UK population in 1700.
- **B** The UK population in 1951 was greater than the UK population in 1901.

23 Which TWO of the following former colonies were granted independence in 1947?

- **A** Pakistan
- **B** Sierra Leone
- **C** Jamaica
- **D** Ceylon (now Sri Lanka)

24 Which famous religious building has been the coronation church since 1066 and is the final resting place for 17 monarchs?

- **A** Westminster Abbey
- **B** York Minster
- **C** St Paul's Cathedral
- **D** Westminster Cathedral

ANSWERS: PRACTICE TEST 14

			Study material reference
1	B	Getting paid	p144–6
2	B	The automatic right to sit in the House of Lords	p111
3	C	Edward	p23
4	A	A postal ballot	p121
5	B	False	p129
6	B	False	p41
7	C	The judiciary	p129–30
8	D	France	p38–9
9	B	The National Assembly for Wales and the Welsh government are based in Cardiff.	p116–7
10	A	The Commonwealth is a group of countries which support each other and work together.	p123–4
11	B	False	p74–5
12	C	Stories about the Bible and saints	p19–21
13	B	False	p13–5
14	A	True	p37
15	A	Yes, except as candidates for the House of Commons	p121–2
16	A	The National Trust	p94
17	C	Traditional English folk music	p79–81
18	A	It was reduced	p22–4
19	B	False	p131
20	B	Canada	p35–7
	C	India	
21	B	False	p17
22	B	The UK population in 1951 was greater than the UK population in 1901.	p64–5
23	A	Pakistan	p52–3
	D	Ceylon (now Sri Lanka)	
24	A	Westminster Abbey	p68

PRACTICE TEST 15

1 During the 19th century, which sector of the Irish economy supported around two-thirds of its people?

- **A** Tourism
- **B** Farming
- **C** Manufacturing
- **D** Shipbuilding

2 Which of the following statements is correct?

- **A** During the Elizabethan period, English settlers began to colonise America.
- **B** During the Elizabethan period, English settlers began to colonise Australia.

3 Which TWO of the following factors contributed to the Industrial Revolution in Britain?

- **A** The foundation of the modern welfare state
- **B** The development of steam power and machinery
- **C** The outbreak of plague
- **D** The repealing of the Corn Laws

4 Which of the following statements is correct?

- **A** The Beveridge Report of 1942 outlined a plan to end the war in Europe.
- **B** The Beveridge Report of 1942 provided the basis of the modern welfare state.

5 By 1200, the English ruled an area of Ireland around Dublin known as what?

- **A** The Pate
- **B** The Pict
- **C** The Pale
- **D** The Plain

6 Official reports of parliamentary proceeding are published in which of the following?

- **A** *The BBC magazine*
- **B** *Hansard*
- **C** *The Telegraph*
- **D** *The Sunday Times*

7 Which of these sectors was NOT nationalised by the post-war Labour government?

- **A** Coal mining
- **B** The railways
- **C** Gas, electric and water supplies
- **D** Farming

8 James II invaded Ireland in an attempt to regain the throne with an army from which country?

- **A** Germany
- **B** France
- **C** Scotland
- **D** Wales

9 Which of these statements is correct?

- **A** You will need the help of a lawyer to issue a small claim.
- **B** You do not need the help of a lawyer to issue a small claim.

10 Following the introduction of the Bill of Rights, monarchs were required to ask Parliament to renew funding for which TWO of the following each year?

- **A** Army
- **B** Building of castles
- **C** Palaces
- **D** Navy

11 Why were more castles built in Britain and Ireland in the Middle Ages?

- **A** They were cheap to build
- **B** They were defensive strongholds
- **C** They were status symbols for the nobility
- **D** They created work for tradesmen

12 Which of the following statements is correct?

- **A** 11 November commemorates soldiers who died in the First World War as well as those who have died in all conflicts involving the UK since then.
- **B** 11 November only commemorates soldiers who died in the First World War.

13 Is this statement TRUE or FALSE?
In Wales and Northern Ireland the established Churches are respectively the Church of Wales and the Church of Ulster.

- **A** True
- **B** False

14 Is the statement below TRUE or FALSE?
The BBC began the world's first regular television service in 1936.

- **A** True
- **B** False

15 Is the statement below TRUE or FALSE?
The Archbishop of Canterbury opens the Parliamentary session each year.

A True

B False

16 Which artist is considered to be the one who raised the profile of landscape painting?

A John Constable

B Thomas Gainsborough

C David Allan

D Joseph Turner

17 The British Broadcasting Corporation (BBC) is funded through television licences. How are the majority of other television channels primarily funded?

A Though a share of the television licence revenue

B Through sponsorship by large national and multinational companies

C Through advertising revenue

D By the government

18 Which of the following is a famous tennis tournament played in the UK every year?

A Wimbledon

B The Grand National

C The Open

D Six Nations

19 Which of the following statements is correct?

A Margaret Thatcher was the longest-serving Prime Minister of the UK in the 20th century.

B Margaret Thatcher was the second longest-serving Prime Minister of the UK in the 20th century.

20 What happened when Charles I tried to impose a revised Prayer Book onto the Presbyterian Church in Scotland?

- **A** The Scottish rebelled and formed an army
- **B** It was very popular across the Union
- **C** It was accepted after some amendments
- **D** The Pope came to England to help Charles I

21 Can young people in every part of the UK volunteer with the National Citizen Service?

- **A** Yes, but each part of the UK has a different website for information about the service
- **B** No, only young people resident in England can volunteer

22 St George is the patron saint of which UK country?

- **A** England
- **B** Scotland
- **C** Wales
- **D** Northern Ireland

23 Is the statement below TRUE or FALSE?
The American colonies rebelled against the British Parliament in the 18th century because they didn't want to pay taxes without representation in Parliament.

- **A** True
- **B** False

24 Which of the following countries does NOT belong to the Commonwealth?

- **A** Canada
- **B** Germany
- **C** Cameroon
- **D** Singapore

ANSWERS: PRACTICE TEST 15

			Study material reference
1	B	Farming	p43
2	A	During the Elizabethan period, English settlers began to colonise America.	p25–6
3	B	The development of steam power and machinery	p35–7
	D	The repealing of the Corn Laws	
4	B	The Beveridge Report of 1942 provided the basis of the modern welfare state.	p53
5	C	The Pale	p17
6	B	*Hansard*	p119
7	D	Farming	p52–3
8	B	France	p31–2
9	B	You do not need the help of a lawyer to issue a small claim.	p133
10	A	Army	p33
	D	Navy	
11	B	They were defensive strongholds	p19–21
12	A	11 November commemorates soldiers who died in the First World War as well as those who have died in all conflicts involving the UK since then.	p72
13	B	False	p67
14	A	True	p48
15	B	False	p107–9
16	D	Joseph Turner	p83
17	C	Through advertising revenue	p92–3
18	A	Wimbledon	p78
19	A	Margaret Thatcher was the longest-serving Prime Minister of the UK in the 20th century.	p58
20	A	The Scottish rebelled and formed an army	p28
21	A	Yes, but each part of the UK has a different website for information about the service	p144–6
22	A	England	p67–8
23	A	True	p38
24	B	Germany	p123–4

PRACTICE TEST 16

1 Some people in Britain were opposed to the slave trade. Who set up the first formal anti-slavery groups in the late 1700s?

- **A** Methodists
- **B** Mormons
- **C** Quakers
- **D** Puritans

2 What is the capital city of Scotland?

- **A** Edinburgh
- **B** Glasgow
- **C** Dundee
- **D** Aberdeen

3 The Elizabethan period in England was a time of growing patriotism. What do we mean by this?

- **A** There was unrest and instability
- **B** The monarchy became unpopular
- **C** The country became more democratic
- **D** A feeling of pride in being English

4 On which day do people send cards to someone they admire, anonymously?

- **A** Christmas Day
- **B** New Year's Day
- **C** Valentine's Day
- **D** April Fool's Day

5 As well as giving legal advice, solicitors are able to do which TWO of the following?

- **A** Represent clients in court
- **B** Arrest suspects
- **C** Take action for a client
- **D** Change the law

6 How many countries belong to the Commonwealth?

- **A** 12
- **B** 25
- **C** 39
- **D** 53

7 Which of the following was NOT a change demanded by the Chartists?

- **A** For elections to be held every five years
- **B** For MPs to be paid
- **C** For ballots to be secret
- **D** For every man to have the vote

8 Which of the following is a document or piece of legislation that sets out fundamental rights or freedoms?

- **A** The UK Constitution
- **B** The Habeas Corpus Act
- **C** The Statute of Rhuddlan
- **D** The Act of Union

9 Is the statement below TRUE or FALSE?
Henry VIII continued his father's work to centralise the administrative powers of England.

- **A** True
- **B** False

10 In which part of the UK was pioneering doctor Alexander Fleming born in 1881?

- **A** Wales
- **B** Scotland
- **C** East Anglia
- **D** Cornwall

11 Which of the following statements is correct?

- **A** At its peak the British Empire had an estimated population of just under 400 million.
- **B** At its peak the British Empire had an estimated population of just under 40 million.

12 In 1913, the British government promised Home Rule for Ireland. Which group within Ireland threatened to resist this move by force?

- **A** The Protestants in the south
- **B** The Muslims in the east
- **C** The Buddhists in the west
- **D** The Protestants in the north

13 Is the statement below TRUE or FALSE?
In 1688, Protestant leaders in England asked William of Orange to invade England and proclaim himself king.

- **A** True
- **B** False

14 Is the statement below TRUE or FALSE?
All MPs represent one of the main political parties.

- **A** True
- **B** False

15 Who were the Picts?

- **A** Ancestors of the Irish people
- **B** Ancestors of the Welsh people
- **C** Ancestors of the Scottish people
- **D** Ancestors of the English people

16 At which of the following famous UK landmarks would you find biomes?

- **A** Giant's Causeway
- **B** The Eden Project
- **C** Snowdonia
- **D** Edinburgh Castle

17 During the English Civil War, in which TWO battles was Charles I's army defeated?

- **A** Battle of Bosworth Field
- **B** Battle of Naseby
- **C** Battle of Marston Moor
- **D** Battle of Hastings

18 Why did Henry VIII marry Anne of Cleves?

- **A** For political reasons
- **B** He loved her
- **C** To have a male heir
- **D** She was beautiful

19 Anyone who wishes to buy tobacco or tobacco products must be over what age?

- **A** 14
- **B** 16
- **C** 18
- **D** 21

20 Which Northern Irish portrait artist, who died in 1941, painted some portraits of the Royal Family?

- **A** Sir John Lavery
- **B** Paul Henry
- **C** Basil Blackshaw
- **D** Markey Robinson

21 Is the statement below TRUE or FALSE?
Charles II was crowned king of England, Wales, Scotland and Ireland in the Restoration after the English Civil War.

- **A** True
- **B** False

22 After Protestants, which is the biggest denomination of Christianity in the UK?

- **A** Jehovah's Witnesses
- **B** Roman Catholic
- **C** Ethiopian Orthodox
- **D** Christian Science

23 Who introduced a system called feudalism to Britain?

- **A** Vikings
- **B** Jutes
- **C** Normans
- **D** Anglo-Saxons

24 Pumpkins, lit with candles, are used to celebrate which tradition?

- **A** Bonfire Night
- **B** Halloween
- **C** Midsummer
- **D** Mayday

ANSWERS: PRACTICE TEST 16

			Study material reference
1	C	Quakers	p37–8
2	A	Edinburgh	p63
3	D	A feeling of pride in being English	p25–6
4	C	Valentine's Day	p72
5	A	Represent clients in court	p134–5
	C	Take action for a client	
6	D	53	p123–4
7	A	For elections to be held every five years	p106
8	B	The Habeas Corpus Act	p135–6
9	A	True	p22–4
10	B	Scotland	p52
11	A	At its peak the British Empire had an estimated population of just under 400 million.	p41
12	D	The Protestants in the north	p47–8
13	A	True	p31–2
14	B	False	p114
15	C	Ancestors of the Scottish people	p13
16	B	The Eden Project	p95–103
17	B	Battle of Naseby	p28–30
	C	Battle of Marston Moor	
18	A	For political reasons	p23
19	C	18	p126–7
20	A	Sir John Lavery	p83
21	A	True	p30
22	B	Roman Catholic	p67
23	C	Normans	p17–8
24	B	Halloween	p72

PRACTICE TEST 17

1 When William of Orange came to the throne with his wife Mary, this later became known as the Glorious Revolution. Why?

- **A** It signalled the start of the Hundred Years War
- **B** William of Orange defeated a much larger army
- **C** It led to the Reformation and the formation of the Protestant Church
- **D** There was no fighting in England

2 Which of the following statements is correct?

- **A** During the reign of Charles I, Parliament attempted to take control of the English army following a rebellion in Ireland.
- **B** During the reign of Charles I, Irish Catholics supported the views of the Puritans.

3 Which political party was Clement Attlee a member of?

- **A** Liberal Democrats
- **B** Conservative
- **C** Green
- **D** Labour

4 A conflict in which of these areas in the 1990s involved British troops?

- **A** The Maldives
- **B** The former Republic of Yugoslavia
- **C** The Baltic states
- **D** Lapland

5 Is the statement below TRUE or FALSE?
There are no differences between the court systems of England, Northern Ireland, Scotland and Wales.

- **A** True
- **B** False

6 Which of the following statements is correct?

- **A** By 1400, in England, official documents were being written in English and English was the preferred language of Parliament and the royal court.
- **B** By 1400, a mixture of Norman French and Anglo-Saxon was being spoken and no unified language was emerging.

7 George and Robert Stephenson are famous for pioneering what?

- **A** The railway engine
- **B** The aeroplane
- **C** The telephone
- **D** The electric lightbulb

8 Is the statement below TRUE or FALSE?
Protestants believed that a person's own relationship with God was more important than submitting to the authority of the Church.

- **A** True
- **B** False

9 Which of the following statements is correct?

- **A** Completed ballots must be handed to an election official.
- **B** Completed ballots must be placed in a ballot box.

10 Which TWO of the following are British inventions?

- **A** Jet engine
- **B** Helicopter
- **C** Golf cart
- **D** Hovercraft

11 Is the statement below TRUE or FALSE?
In the UK, everybody has the right to choose their religion or choose not to practise a religion.

A True

B False

12 Is the statement below TRUE or FALSE?
The language of the Iron Age was part of the Celtic language family.

A True

B False

13 When England became a republic, after Charles I lost the English Civil War, it no longer had what?

A A parliament

B A national anthem

C A monarch

D A Prime Minister

14 Is the statement below TRUE or FALSE?
In 1690, following his unsuccessful attempt to regain his throne in Ireland, James II fled back to the Netherlands.

A True

B False

15 Income tax is NOT paid on which of the following forms of income?

A Pension

B Money you win on the lottery

C Benefits

D All of the above

16 Which of the following statements is correct?

- **A** The small claims procedure is an informal way of helping people who have been victims of identity theft or fraud.
- **B** The small claims procedure is an informal way of helping people settle minor disputes without needing a lawyer.

17 Which of the following is a British invention or innovation?

- **A** A Turing machine
- **B** Micro Machines
- **C** The telephone
- **D** The photocopier

18 Is the statement below TRUE or FALSE?
It is possible to find information about visiting Parliament on the UK Parliament website.

- **A** True
- **B** False

19 Is the statement below TRUE or FALSE?
The Houses of Parliament were built in the 19th century when the medieval 'gothic' style of architecture was popular.

- **A** True
- **B** False

20 The Elizabeth Tower is part of which building in London?

- **A** St Paul's Cathedral
- **B** Houses of Parliament
- **C** Mansion House
- **D** Buckingham Palace

21 Is it possible for the leader of the opposition to become Prime Minister?

- **A** Yes, if the Prime Minister resigns
- **B** Yes, if his or her party wins a General Election

22 People usually spend Christmas Day at home and enjoy a special meal that normally includes Christmas pudding, mince pies and which meat?

- **A** Duck
- **B** Turkey
- **C** Guinea fowl
- **D** Pork

23 Which TWO of the following describe the purpose of the UN Security Council?

- **A** To promote human rights
- **B** To recommend action during an international crisis
- **C** To recommend action where there is a threat to peace
- **D** To make international law

24 Which Acts of Parliament, passed in 1832 and 1867, abolished rotten boroughs, gave more parliamentary seats to urban areas and greatly increased the right of people to vote?

- **A** The Change Acts
- **B** The Voting Acts
- **C** The Election Acts
- **D** The Reform Acts

ANSWERS: PRACTICE TEST 17

			Study material reference
1	D	There was no fighting in England	p31–2
2	A	During the reign of Charles I, Parliament attempted to take control of the English army following a rebellion in Ireland.	p28
3	D	Labour	p53
4	B	The former Republic of Yugoslavia	p59–60
5	B	False	p130–3
6	A	By 1400, in England, official documents were being written in English and English was the preferred language of Parliament and the royal court.	p19–21
7	A	The railway engine	p41–2
8	A	True	p22–4
9	B	Completed ballots must be placed in a ballot box.	p121
10	A	Jet engine	p56–7
	D	Hovercraft	
11	A	True	p66
12	A	True	p12–3
13	C	A monarch	p28–30
14	B	False	p31–2
15	B	Money you win on the lottery	p137–8
16	B	The small claims procedure is an informal way of helping people settle minor disputes without needing a lawyer.	p133
17	A	A Turing machine	p56–7
18	A	True	p122–3
19	A	True	p84–5
20	B	Houses of Parliament	p95–103
21	B	Yes, if his or her party wins a General Election	p114
22	B	Turkey	p69–70
23	B	To recommend action during an international crisis	p125
	C	To recommend action where there is a threat to peace	
24	D	The Reform Acts	p43–4

PRACTICE TEST 18

1 Police forces are headed by whom?

- **A** Ministers
- **B** Generals
- **C** Mayors
- **D** Chief Constables

2 Is the statement below TRUE or FALSE?
A Formula 1 Grand Prix race is held in Britain every year.

- **A** True
- **B** False

3 Which of the following can volunteers help in?

- **A** Air raid shelters
- **B** Homeless shelters
- **C** Life in the UK test centres
- **D** Juries

4 During the 1960s, Parliament passed new laws that made it illegal for employers to discriminate against women because of their gender and gave them which right?

- **A** Free lunches
- **B** Equal pay
- **C** Childcare at work
- **D** Two years' maternity leave

5 Who wrote the piece of music, *Belshazzar's Feast*?

- **A** Henry Purcell
- **B** Sir William Walton
- **C** Gustav Holst
- **D** Sir Edward Elgar

6 Is the statement below TRUE or FALSE?
The 1950s was a time of serious unrest in Northern Ireland.

- **A** True
- **B** False

7 The UK joined which international organisation in 1973?

- **A** The UN
- **B** NATO
- **C** The Commonwealth
- **D** The EEC

8 Mary Stuart was forced to flee to England after being accused of murder. Who was she accused of murdering?

- **A** Her father
- **B** Her husband
- **C** Her brother
- **D** Her sister

9 Which of these countries did NOT fight on the side of the Allied Powers during the First World War?

- **A** Bulgaria
- **B** Italy
- **C** USA
- **D** Serbia

10 King Edward I of England annexed Wales to the crown of England by which statute?

- **A** The Statute of Caernarfon
- **B** The Statute of Gwynedd
- **C** The Statute of Carmarthen
- **D** The Statute of Rhuddlan

11 Where in London is the White Tower?

- **A** Tower of London
- **B** Buckingham Palace
- **C** Palace of Westminster
- **D** St Paul's Cathedral

12 Is the statement below TRUE or FALSE?
The Reformation failed in Scotland and the country remained strongly Catholic.

- **A** True
- **B** False

13 How did Jane Seymour die?

- **A** Following childbirth
- **B** She was executed
- **C** Old age
- **D** The plague

14 Who won the English Civil War in 1646?

- **A** Parliament
- **B** The Cavaliers
- **C** The king
- **D** None of the above

15 What special type of windows did many cathedrals built in the Middle Ages have?

- **A** Arched
- **B** Mullioned
- **C** Stained glass
- **D** Sash

16 Which of the following statements is correct?

- **A** Countries are obliged to belong to the Commonwealth.
- **B** Countries join the Commonwealth voluntarily.

17 Which TWO of the following names may be given to the day before Lent starts?

- **A** Ash Wednesday
- **B** Shrove Tuesday
- **C** Good Friday
- **D** Pancake Day

18 Sir Chris Hoy is a famous sportsman in which event or sport?

- **A** Athletics
- **B** Ice skating
- **C** Swimming
- **D** Cycling

19 Which English king led his army to victory at the Battle of Agincourt?

- **A** Henry V
- **B** Henry VII
- **C** Henry II
- **D** Henry VIII

20 During the 17th century, many people left Britain and Ireland to settle in which of the following places?

- **A** France
- **B** Africa
- **C** America
- **D** London

21 Is the statement below TRUE or FALSE?
It is legal to carry a weapon if it is for self-defence.

A True

B False

22 There was growth in British film, fashion and music during the 1960s. Which TWO of these were very popular sixties British pop groups?

A ABBA

B The Beatles

C The Rolling Stones

D The Beach Boys

23 Is the statement below TRUE or FALSE?
Income tax pays for services such as education, roads and the armed services.

A True

B False

24 Fighting broke out between colonists in North America and British forces in the late 18th century. What did thirteen colonies declare in 1776?

A Defeat

B Surrender

C Independence

D An alliance

ANSWERS: PRACTICE TEST 18

			Study material reference
1	D	Chief Constables	p127–8
2	A	True	p78
3	B	Homeless shelters	p144–6
4	B	Equal pay	p55
5	B	Sir William Walton	p79–81
6	B	False	p57
7	D	The EEC	p124–5
8	B	Her husband	p25
9	A	Bulgaria	p46–7
10	D	The Statute of Rhuddlan	p17
11	A	Tower of London	p84–5
12	B	False	p25
13	A	Following childbirth	p23
14	A	Parliament	p28–30
15	C	Stained glass	p19–21
16	B	Countries join the Commonwealth voluntarily.	p123–4
17	B	Shrove Tuesday	p69–70
	D	Pancake Day	
18	D	Cycling	p74–5
19	A	Henry V	p17
20	C	America	p34
21	B	False	p126–7
22	B	The Beatles	p55
	C	The Rolling Stones	
23	A	True	p137–8
24	C	Independence	p38

PRACTICE TEST 19

1 Who was Cnut (Canute)?

- **A** A Danish king of England
- **B** An Anglo-Saxon king of England
- **C** A Scottish lord
- **D** A Viking warrior

2 Who is NOT appointed to the cabinet?

- **A** The Chancellor of the Exchequer
- **B** The Speaker
- **C** The Foreign Secretary
- **D** The Home Secretary

3 Scotland developed its own Parliament. This was divided into three parts. What were they called?

- **A** The lords, the commons and the clergy
- **B** The lords, the commons and the Estates
- **C** The lords, the commons and the Houses
- **D** The lords, the commons and the bishops

4 Is the statement below TRUE or FALSE?
English laws and the English language were introduced to Wales during the Middle Ages.

- **A** True
- **B** False

5 Is the statement below TRUE or FALSE?
The Council of Europe is another name for the European Union.

- **A** True
- **B** False

6 Which of the following is the title of the David Lean directed film of 1962?

- **A** *Lawrence of Asia*
- **B** *Lawrence of Australia*
- **C** *Lawrence of Amsterdam*
- **D** *Lawrence of Arabia*

7 Looking after the environment involves which TWO of the following?

- **A** Buying new products whenever possible
- **B** Buying recycled products whenever possible
- **C** Recycling waste when possible
- **D** Using more energy when possible

8 It is enshrined in law that men and women in the UK have equal rights to work, own property, marry and which of the following?

- **A** Divorce
- **B** Cook meals
- **C** Travel abroad
- **D** Own a dog

9 The Scottish Parliament has how many members?

- **A** 60
- **B** 108
- **C** 129
- **D** 360

10 Who were the Jutes, Angles and Saxons?

- **A** Tribespeople from northern Europe
- **B** Romans
- **C** Tribespeople from Wales
- **D** Tribespeople from Scotland

11 Which country's coastline did James Cook map, leading to the establishment of colonies there?

- **A** Indonesia
- **B** Portugal
- **C** South Africa
- **D** Australia

12 About which conflict did poets Wilfred Owen and Siegfried Sassoon write?

- **A** Crimean War
- **B** Boer War
- **C** First World War
- **D** Second World War

13 Which Jewish religious festival happens in November or December every year?

- **A** Eid al-Fitr
- **B** Eid ul Adha
- **C** Hannukah
- **D** Vaisakhi

14 The 'Ashes' are played for between England and Australia in which sport?

- **A** Rugby union
- **B** Tennis
- **C** Darts
- **D** Cricket

15 Which of the following statements is correct?

- **A** Mary, Queen of Scots hoped Elizabeth I might help her regain her throne.
- **B** Mary, Queen of Scots had no faith that Elizabeth I might help her.

16 How are people chosen for a jury?

- **A** Randomly, from the electoral register
- **B** Randomly, from the lottery
- **C** People apply to be on a jury
- **D** They are appointed by legal professionals

17 Cowes on the Isle of Wight is most famous in a sporting context for which of the following?

- **A** Rowing
- **B** Sailing
- **C** Fishing championships
- **D** Surfing

18 How old must you be to drive a car or motorcycle?

- **A** 16
- **B** 17
- **C** 25
- **D** 70

19 Is the statement below TRUE or FALSE?
Employees need to pay National Insurance Contributions themselves.

- **A** True
- **B** False

20 Which of these is NOT a famous poet?

- **A** William Wordsworth
- **B** Alfred Lord Tennyson
- **C** Percy Shelley
- **D** Lucian Freud

21 Which of James II's relatives were strictly Protestant?

- **A** Brothers
- **B** Sisters
- **C** Daughters
- **D** Aunts and uncles

22 Which TWO of the following are responsibilities for members of Parliament (MPs)?

- **A** To represent everyone in their constituency
- **B** To support all government decisions and laws
- **C** To scrutinise and comment on the government's activities
- **D** To only represent constituents who voted for them

23 Pressure and lobby groups represent the interests of which TWO of the following?

- **A** Minor political parties
- **B** Foreign ambassadors
- **C** Business organisations
- **D** Campaigning organisations

24 Is the following statement TRUE or FALSE?
***The title of the UK national anthem is* 'Long Live the Queen'.**

- **A** True
- **B** False

ANSWERS: PRACTICE TEST 19

			Study material reference
1	A	A Danish king of England	p15
2	B	The Speaker	p113–4
3	A	The lords, the commons and the clergy	p18–9
4	A	True	p17
5	B	False	p125
6	D	*Lawrence of Arabia*	p91
7	B	Buying recycled products whenever possible	p146
	C	Recycling waste when possible	
8	A	Divorce	p65–6
9	C	129	p118
10	A	Tribespeople from northern Europe	p13–5
11	D	Australia	p35–7
12	C	First World War	p86–8
13	C	Hannukah	p70–1
14	D	Cricket	p76
15	A	Mary, Queen of Scots hoped Elizabeth I might help her regain her throne.	p25
16	A	Randomly, from the electoral register	p130
17	B	Sailing	p78
18	B	17	p139
19	B	False	p138–9
20	D	Lucian Freud	p83
21	C	Daughters	p31
22	A	To represent everyone in their constituency	p110
	C	To scrutinise and comment on the government's activities	
23	C	Business organisations	p114
	D	Campaigning organisations	
24	B	False	p109

PRACTICE TEST 20

1 Is the statement below TRUE or FALSE?
The Scottish Exhibition and Conference Centre is in Edinburgh.

- **A** True
- **B** False

2 Which TWO of the following are famous plays by William Shakespeare?

- **A** *The Duchess of Malfi*
- **B** *Romeo and Juliet*
- **C** *A Midsummer Night's Dream*
- **D** *Dr Faustus*

3 In which British city is the Royal Crescent?

- **A** Bath
- **B** Exeter
- **C** Edinburgh
- **D** Cardiff

4 During which period of the Christian calendar is it traditional to fast?

- **A** Easter
- **B** Christmas
- **C** Lent
- **D** Advent

5 By the middle of the 15th century, what had happened to the last of the Welsh rebellions?

- **A** They had been defeated by the English
- **B** They had been contained within Wales
- **C** They were victorious over the English armies
- **D** They were abandoned because they were too expensive

6 Which British Admiral was killed at the Battle of Trafalgar?

- **A** Napoleon
- **B** Nelson
- **C** Sir Francis Drake
- **D** Duke of Wellington

7 Which of the following statements is correct?

- **A** Civil law relates to crimes which are investigated by the police.
- **B** Civil law relates to disputes between people.

8 Who was responsible for building the Tower of London?

- **A** William the Conqueror
- **B** Edward I
- **C** Henry VIII
- **D** Elizabeth I

9 Who was the first Briton to win the Tour de France?

- **A** Sir Chris Hoy
- **B** Sir Bradley Wiggins
- **C** Mark Cavendish
- **D** Reg Harris

10 Is it legal to send a girl abroad for circumcision or cutting?

- **A** Yes, if it is legal in the country to which she is sent
- **B** No, it is illegal in the UK to send a girl abroad for circumcision or cutting

11 Is the statement below TRUE or FALSE?
The Council of Europe has the power to make laws which are binding in member states.

- **A** True
- **B** False

12 William Beveridge briefly served as an MP and was subsequently leader in the House of Lords for which political party?

A The Labour Party

B The Liberal Party

C The Conservative Party

D The Green Party

13 Halloween is regarded historically as which of the following?

A A Christian festival

B A Muslim festival

C A pagan festival

D A Sikh festival

14 Where in Ireland did the English government encourage Scottish and English Protestants to settle during the reigns of Elizabeth I and James I?

A Ulster

B Dublin

C Cork

D Armagh

15 A famous boat race for rowers is contested on the River Thames each year between which university teams?

A Cambridge and London

B Edinburgh and Oxford

C Edinburgh and London

D Cambridge and Oxford

16 Penicillin was developed into a usable drug by Howard Florey and which other scientist?

- **A** Stephen Hawking
- **B** Marie Curie
- **C** Albert Einstein
- **D** Ernst Chain

17 Which artist, born in 1937, is famous for his contribution to the 'pop art' movement of the 1960s?

- **A** Lucian Freud
- **B** John Petts
- **C** David Hockney
- **D** Robert Lenkiewicz

18 Members of the Northern Ireland Assembly have worked together successfully since which year?

- **A** 2000
- **B** 2003
- **C** 2007
- **D** 2011

19 Which of these is NOT a UK regional language?

- **A** Welsh
- **B** Irish Gaelic
- **C** Gaelic
- **D** Kentish

20 Which of the statements below is NOT correct?

- **A** More women than men study at university.
- **B** There are now more female MPs than male MPs.
- **C** Employment opportunities for women are much greater than they were in the past.
- **D** Women work in all sectors of the economy.

21 Is the statement below TRUE or FALSE?
Ellie Simmonds is a Paralympian and was the youngest member of the British team at the 2008 games.

- **A** True
- **B** False

22 Is the statement below TRUE or FALSE?
Hospitals often need donated blood to help people who are ill or injured.

- **A** True
- **B** False

23 In the Church of Scotland, who is the Moderator?

- **A** A key figure who is responsible for all relations with the Church of England.
- **B** A financial overseer who has overall responsibility for the accounts of the Church.
- **C** The spiritual leader of the Church, who is appointed for life.
- **D** The chairperson of the General Assembly, who is appointed for one year only and often speaks on behalf of the Church.

24 Emmeline Pankhurst, who was born in Manchester in 1858, had a role in establishing which TWO organisations for women's rights?

- **A** The Women's Voting Council
- **B** The Women's Franchise League
- **C** The Female Democratic Organisation
- **D** The Women's Social and Political Union

ANSWERS: PRACTICE TEST 20

			Study material reference
1	B	False	p79–81
2	B	*Romeo and Juliet*	p26
	C	*A Midsummer Night's Dream*	
3	A	Bath	p84–5
4	C	Lent	p69–70
5	A	They had been defeated by the English	p17
6	B	Nelson	p38–9
7	B	Civil law relates to disputes between people.	p126–7
8	A	William the Conqueror	p95-103
9	B	Sir Bradley Wiggins	p74–5
10	B	No, it is illegal in the UK to send a girl abroad for circumcision or cutting	p137
11	B	False	p125
12	B	The Liberal Party	p53
13	C	A pagan festival	p72
14	A	Ulster	p27
15	D	Cambridge and Oxford	p78
16	D	Ernst Chain	p52
17	C	David Hockney	p83
18	C	2007	p118–9
19	D	Kentish	p64
20	B	There are now more female MPs than male MPs.	p65–6
21	A	True	p74–5
22	A	True	p144
23	D	The chairperson of the General Assembly, who is appointed for one year only and often speaks on behalf of the Church.	p67
24	B	The Women's Franchise League	p44
	D	The Women's Social and Political Union	

You've just taken 20 full tests.

Best of luck for your official Life in the UK test.

Let us know how it goes at
www.lifeintheuk.net/feedback

We'd love to hear your experiences, good or bad, or any suggestions you have to help us make our products better.